THE SINGING LAND

THE SINGING LAND

22
natural environments of Australia
from surging ocean to arid desert

VINCENT SERVENTY

Charles Scribner's Sons • New York

Library of Congress Catalog Card Number 73-1596
SBN 684-13369-5

Printed in Hong Kong

CONTENTS

The singing land

This land, Australia, is to me a singing land. For three million square miles its rich diversity arises—in the song of birds, the croaking of frogs, the dissonance of some of the marsupials; but it is also *a singing land* in the living composition of its landforms, plants and wildlife.

This vast land is under attack from man, who destroys his own home, his own living place. Tractors and bulldozers tear at the ocean beaches, and destroy the forests.

Many of the attacks are needless and harmful, and made by those who have not yet begun to consider their environment as a whole. With greater knowledge man can avoid disastrous mistakes, and laboriously reverse some of the mistakes of the past.

In *Landforms of Australia* I tried to unfold a greater interest and understanding by showing something of the shaping of the land. In *Dryandra* I tried to show the interweavings of life, both in space and time, in one small region of forest country. In this book I have broadened the task to look at the land and life over the whole of Australia.

I have not intended to present every type of environment or an *exact* study of environments in Australia—just those I know best, covering most of the major habitats of the continent.

If a traveller starts from the ocean and, after landing on a beach, journeys to the centre of the continent, he passes from the plants of the sand dunes, through a range of formations into dense rainforest. Then the forest becomes more and more open, with occasional vestiges of rainforest. On the western plains the trees become smaller, and shrubs take their place, with increasing grasslands and soon stony deserts. No straight line would give this exact pattern, but all can be found in a less precise journey. Going farther west, the patterns appear in reverse, from desert through to coastal dune, though rainforests do not grow here.

The Singing Land has been formed on such an imaginary journey. Alpine and other special lands are described at the end of the book.

Any classification is of course only a convenient box; and often it is hard to decide which form is which. Experts differ on the names to be used. One formation merges into another, as changes continually take place through fire or animal action, or the hand of man, or because of long-term changes in climate. The basic control of the plants is through climate, especially rainfall; but there are other strong factors such as soil, aspect, and even geological history.

In the varying habitats live many animals, some found all the time, some visitors on a regular pattern each year, some only occasional stragglers. One easily understood method in describing the plant life is to classify the formations by their "look". Mangroves, woodland, rainforest have the same character the world over, even though the plants and animals may vary from one country to another. I have used such groupings, and described the life most commonly found in them, with stress on how plants and animals have adapted themselves to these particular environments.

1
start of the food chain
SURGING OCEAN

We call our home planet Earth. Yet if we can ever communicate with those marine brothers of man, the dolphins, they will claim that Oceanus is the correct name, for seventy per cent of the surface of the globe is covered with water. Our own bodies hold the same percentage of water. Solids, whether of body or earth, are the smaller part.

The depths of the oceans at 36,000 feet would swallow the heights of earth—Mount Everest at 29,000 feet. For the purposes of this book the oceans will be considered only in terms of the flotsam which washes up on our beaches and occasional ocean wanderers, the deepwater swimmers that visit our coast.

The vast mass of the oceans teems with life. All the plants and animals that float in the waters and drift at the mercy of the winds and currents are collectively called the plankton. Sixty per cent are diatoms, microscopic algae. Since "all flesh is grass" the diatoms are the base of the pyramid of life. There are larger algae, the seaweeds, with which we are more familiar, and many float on the surface by the aid of small bladders.

At times stirring of the waters by storms, upwelling currents and increasing sunlight in spring cause an outburst of growth. Then the sea becomes coloured brown or green with the myriad microscopic plants. Browsing among this feast of diatoms are the microscopic animals and also plant-animals, which have some of the qualities of both. This animal life has a bewildering variety. Some are adult and microscopic, others are larval forms of animals which will one day become sea urchins, crabs, fish or some other well-known marine creature. Elaborate food chains are built up beginning with the diatoms. At the other end of the chain may be giant fish like the basking shark, or blue whale; or else the wandering albatross.

Besides the planktonic life of the surface layers where sunlight can penetrate, there is also a wealth of life which lives on the bottoms of the shallow seas of the continental shelf. More bizarre though less frequent are the animals which creep on the floor of the ocean depths. Above these animals of the sea bottom, are the active swimmers which can feed in the surface layers or dive deep to feed on bottom-living animals.

Here we will look at just a few of the animals that come from the oceans beyond our shores. Because of the spin of the earth, the pull of sun and moon, and the unequal heating from the sun at equator and poles, the oceans of water move in slow swirls, just as the vast reaches of air are moved, faster, by the same powers. Movements of water tend to follow those of wind.

For Australia the pattern is broadly that on the southern coastline the wind drift from the west, sweeping round the globe in the Roaring Forties, brings dwellers of the sub-Antarctic to our shores. Some are migrants heading south, though at times blown even westwards. This cold current sweeps up the west coast and keeps seas beyond Perth colder than those on the east coast. A warm tropical current, the south equinoctial current, swings from New Caledonia towards Australia and then moves south. Also southward-flowing is the East Australian current, which after warming southeastern Australia swings towards New Zealand. The

Timor current pours westwards along the northern coastline. There are seasonal variations on these movements, but that is the picture in broad outline.

The kind of life which comes from the seas to our shores can be more tropical or more temperate than the latitudes might suggest.

One example may show the effect of the currents on sea life—that of the Australian salmon, as given by Dr Bruce Malcolm in *The Fisherman*. In outline, and accepting that we still do not know enough of the life history to be dogmatic, this is the story:

The Australian salmon is not a true salmon but, relished by early settlers, it earned that name. In our waters there are two main kinds, the western and the eastern. Salmon have structures called "rakers" on the first gill arch, and these can be used as strainers for catching planktonic life. The eastern form, which feeds mainly on plankton, has a larger number of rakers than the western, which hunts small fish.

The western form is found in southern and southwestern waters; the eastern occurs north to Sydney. In the waters of Victoria and Tasmania the groups mix.

In April and May the western form spawn around Cape Leeuwin. The youngsters probably drift slowly eastwards on the west wind drift. Two-inch long fish are found in Tasmanian waters about five to six months later. The fish stay in the southeastern corner until they are almost adult at about five years of age. Then they move westwards ready in turn for their spawning.

For the eastern form the migration journey is not so long. Spawning takes place in summer in southern New South Wales, and the young drift south on the East Australian current. At four to five years old the juveniles move north once more to spawn. Scientists think this is the most probable pattern of life for the western and eastern forms of the Australian salmon.

No doubt equally fascinating, though as yet still not worked out, could be the migration of our eels. The dramatic story of eel movements from Europe across the Atlantic to the West Indies is well known. Gilbert Whitley says that northwestern Australian eels possibly breed in Indonesia, and the eastern Australian species may go to New Caledonia to breed.

Another ocean wanderer of the warmer Atlantic, Indian and Pacific oceans is the whale shark, which may grow to fifty feet long and reach several tons—the world's largest shark, yet it is harmless to man. Though the head is broad and blunt, with thousands of small teeth in the jaws, its food is gathered by gill structures which strain out planktonic life. The number of sightings indicate that it visits Australian shores quite frequently.

Another regular visitor is the sunfish. This extraordinary creature belongs to the same group as the toadoes, porcupine fishes, leatherjackets and trigger fishes; but the sunfish is the giant. Adult sunfish can weigh more than a ton and reach a length of eight to ten feet. However, in width they are only a few feet, and in girth may reach nearly twenty-six feet—truly a giant among fish. The rounded shape is similar to that of the old fashioned millstone, and early scientists gave the sunfish the name *mola*, which in Latin means millstone.

Many naturalists and travellers have told how at times sunfish will gather in small groups lying lazily on the surface of the ocean. To get the full benefit of the warmth the fish lies on its side. The fins on this fish are as strange as its shape. The back and keel fins are almost equal in size and opposite each other. Gilbert Whitley tells how these fish swim by sculling with their body. The long fins twist slightly, producing a similar action to that of a ship's propeller. The arm fins are tiny and the tail fin almost nothing. However, the sunfish seems to have little fear of enemies, and is easily caught. Its defence lies in its huge size and an extraordinarily thick skin. Under the outer layer is a plate of hard gristle about two to three inches in thickness. Whitley describes this layer as so tough it can turn bullets fired from a rifle.

A female sunfish, when cut open, was found to contain 300,000,000 eggs, not yet developed; this shows the egg-laying capacity of the mother. The babies when hatched at the sea surface are tiny, about a twelfth of an inch long. These look a little like toadoes. When a little older they look like tiny porcupine fish with spikes in all directions. Five of the spikes grow into larger horns; all this while the youngster is less than half an inch long. It is no wonder these early stages were once regarded as being of entirely different fish. Then the adult shape slowly develops; the tiny scrap of flesh in time becomes a marine giant.

Food of the sunfish is said to consist largely of floating sea-life like jellyfish, shrimps and small fish; the larvae of eels are devoured in great quantities.

One captured sunfish had in its stomach a fish that lives only in the deeper waters of the ocean. Perhaps sunfish can dive at times. In South Africa superstitious fishermen put back to the shore if they meet a sunfish. Legend has it that such a sighting will lead to disaster; the scientist who reports this story also mentions that sunfish do not usually come close inshore except in bad weather, so perhaps there is a good reason for the belief.

A fisherman confronted with something new usually asks, "What is it?" The next question is, "Can you eat it?" The answer here seems to be "Yes". Though many of its relatives are poisonous, the flesh of the sunfish is said to be harmless. Most writers agree it is tough and tasteless. Norman and Fraser in their classic book on giant fishes, whales and dolphins relate that one gentleman whose cook turned some sunfish flesh into soup, tasted it and declared it the "best turtle soup he had tasted for a long time".

Sunfish roam the oceans of the world, and strandings in Australia occur at regular intervals. The giant sunfish has a much smaller relative, the short sunfish; this creature is a pygmy, only three feet long. However, what it loses in bulk it gains in speed, and is said to be a very fast swimmer.

An ocean-going fish, perhaps in earlier times mistaken for a "sea serpent", is the oarfish. The first impression is of an extremely long and thin fish. With a length of twelve feet, the body has a depth of just over one foot, and a thickness of three inches at its widest part. Some animals have been found twenty feet long, and these weigh over a quarter of a ton.

Added to this unusual shape is an unusual fin development. There is no tail fin. The dorsal fin runs the whole length of the body, and at the front rears up in a crest. The pelvic fins are thin and narrow for most of the two feet of their length, but at the tip broaden into small paddles. It is said that these give the name oarfish. Be$_{ing}$ thin and weak such fins would be used only in display and not for swimming. A more likely explanation of the name oarfish is that the whole body is the shape of a giant sweep oar and the resemblance would be seen by fishermen.

Most oarfish come ashore in the early summer months. It is possible they come inshore to breed and may find themselves victim of sudden storms. Judging from the shape of the fish, it could be a poor swimmer, and the few eye witness accounts suggest this. Some have been seen lying on their sides, others swimming with wavelike motions of their long bodies.

How do these large and apparently helpless fish protect themselves? Often they come ashore mutilated; but judging by the reaction of land animals the flesh is not attractive. One observer states that even dogs refuse it, either raw or cooked. Possibly the glittering silver of the body and the flaming red crest is a warning to save the fish from attack.

The silver of the skin is made of small scales of guanin, a waste product of the kidneys, and which by its nature reflects light. A hand rubbed over the body of the fish transfers this silver "paint" quite readily.

The oarfish's rarity and strange appearance has excited curiosity down the ages. The European name of King of the Herrings arose from a belief that the fish came with, or just before, the herring shoals. Any interference with the king would lead to the disappearance of the herrings, a tragedy in those times when food from the sea was the staple diet of the coastal people. Scientists paid tribute to the legend by calling the oarfish *Regalecus*, a combination of king and herring. The Japanese, with more flamboyance, named it *Dugunonatatori*, which means "cock of the palace under the sea".

Is the oarfish the basis for some of the legends of sea monsters? Certainly it would fit many descriptions—a huge snake-like animal with a flaming crest. Professor Wood Jones actually caught a live fish and, even though it was damaged, when prodded it raised the red crest.

Whatever the legend, the truth is strange enough. As the years pass more will be learned of the oarfish, but until then it remains an exciting mystery fish.

There are other bluewater animals. Marine mammals such as whales sometimes come close inshore. The sperm whales normally keep well out in the waters off the continental shelf, but occasionally mass strandings take place. Possibly the whales' sonar becomes baffled by a shelving sandy coastline, and they swim confident they are in open waters, till suddenly the herd is stranded in the shallows. The smaller toothed whales, such as the killer whales, also come inshore, and in earlier times became a legend at Twofold Bay, where these killers helped man to hunt bigger whales. Smaller dolphins and pilot whales even come into estuaries.

The largest of all animals, the whalebone whales, also come inshore on migration. Best known is the humpback, and huge numbers once came from the colder Antarctic waters in winter to give birth to their young in the warmer waters of the northeast and northwest coasts. Ruthless hunting destroyed the herds, and it may take as long as fifty years before the old numbers return.

There are too, the seabirds, wandering albatrosses with the biggest wingspan of all birds, visiting us in winter and at times even venturing into harbours.

Short-tailed shearwaters, better known as the Tasmanian muttonbird, spend the northern summer in the seas off Japan and Alaska, then swing in a huge figure of eight pattern across the Pacific southwards along the east coast in springtime for the nesting islands, mainly in Bass Strait. Nesting over, in autumn, the huge mass of adults and young travels north, once more completing a remarkable flight across the Pacific.

There are gannets from New Zealand fishing the southern coastline, terns of many species, some sedentary, some coming from the northern hemisphere. Even marine turtles visit most waters on their wanderings.

Smaller, are the various animals without backbones, delicate violet snails, barnacles attached to floating logs or bottles, and those remarkable colony-living jellyfish which, drifting before the wind, at times become stranded in countless millions on all the western and eastern coastlines. At sea a ship may sail through huge flotillas of these jellyfish.

In earlier times off the coast of Portugal seamen saw sailing over the surface a small animal with a sausage-shaped float. The long trailing tentacles sting like fire, so the name of Portuguese man-of-war was given. The "broadsides" fired by the stinging cells were warlike enough. Storms often wash these drifters ashore on our east and west coasts. One was found at Macquarie Island, well south of the tropical waters which are its home.

The sail is an airbladder, often twisted into a cockscomb shape, with a kind of crimping along the top edge. Usually the float is coloured in shades of blue and purple, no doubt to help the animal hide on the ocean surface. Below the float are various body parts. Then come the tentacles, which may be ten to twelve feet long. The Portuguese man-of-war belongs to an extraordinary animal group—in which different animals live bonded together for the common good. One makes the float, another the stinging tentacles, and still others the stomach parts.

Cleland and Southcott in their comprehensive book on injuries from marine invertebrates could not find any deaths caused by the stings of Portuguese men-of-war, though they did find some fascinating historical reference to their use as a poison when dried. An unfortunate cook was once hanged for allegedly poisoning his master by making soup which he peppered with dried and powdered Portuguese man-of-war. Farmers of Guadeloupe and Colombia reportedly used the same sort of powder to kill rats. There is, as yet, no conclusive evidence that the man-of-war is poisonous as a food.

Another smaller yet just as beautiful drifter is the sallee rover or by-the-wind sailor. This name refers to the triangular sail which projects from a circular body about the size of a twenty cent piece. Like the man-of-war, each rover is a colony, and the disk contains gas bubbles which keep the colony afloat. Instead of long, trailing, stinging tentacles, these are all short and have no troublesome effect on people. The larvae live in deep water, perhaps three thousand feet below the surface, and are reddish in colour, compared with the ocean blue of the adults.

About the same size, but lacking the sail, is porpita, another relative of the man-of-war, not as common as the other two.

Perhaps we can close this story of animals of the ocean with the life of the goose barnacle. Throughout history barnacles have exasperated man. Sailing ships soon had their bottoms covered with a vigorous marine garden which slowed their progress to a dangerous level. Careening the boat and scraping the hull became a regular job in early times.

Today goose barnacles are often seen attached to floating boxes, old shells and other flotsam that drifts ashore. The goose barnacles have long stalks with, at the end of each, small shelled animals which open when feeding and wave feathery plumes in the water. The plumes resemble bird feathers, and an ancient legend has it that one kind hatches out "barnacle geese" which then live on land.

We now know that barnacles are not molluscs but crustaceans, as the jointed legs indicate. With the feathery strainers these barnacles trap planktonic life. Not all barnacles have stalks. In many the animal fastens itself onto the host, which may be a rock, a ship, a whale, a fish, a turtle or any object in the sea that allows the larval barnacle to gain a foot hold—or rather head hold, since the scientist T. H. Huxley first coined that famous description of the creature as "fixed by its head and kicking the food into its mouth with its legs".

2
garden of animals
CORAL REEF

A coral reef is like a flower garden where all the plants are animals. This is an old comment, and reflects the general impression that such reefs seem to be all animals. Yet there must be plants somewhere in the complex, otherwise animals could not survive. As with the oceans, the plankton is the major supplier of plant food. This crop is uniform the whole year round, without the spring and autumn outbursts of diatom growth of the oceans. Much of the reef has a layer of calcareous algae, and also films of blue green algae. The reason this "lawn" is not obvious is that fish and other animals keep it close-cropped. Protection from grazers allows it to develop a more obvious growth.

The most remarkable of all algae are those that grow in the tissues of reef animals, particularly coral polyps.

In a normal coral colony there is three times as much plant life tissue as animal, and the bulk grows as green strands through the coral skeleton. Some lives in the living flesh of the polyp and, with the aid of sunlight and carbon dioxide, it is able to make fresh growth and give off oxygen which can be used by the polyp. Recent research has shown that the polyps also get food from this "internal garden". This is one reason why reef corals can grow only in the upper levels of the ocean. In the best conditions this can be as deep as 300 feet, but is usually limited to about 180 feet, with more rapid growth in shallower water. The algae, being dependent on sunlight, cannot flourish in the deeper waters where light does not penetrate.

Corals can grow rapidly: 25,000 polyps developed (in one study) in 1000 days. To give some idea of the mass, one lump weighing 15 tons was estimated to have thirty million animals. Such coral, and calcareous algae, together with other reef building life has created the 1,200 miles of the Great Barrier Reef. Here the various structures, fringing reefs, barrier reefs, platform reefs and low islands, enclose 8,000 square miles of sea, with a bewildering variety of animals in this marine wonderland. A few examples will show the variety:

Professor W. Stephenson writes that a university team recorded 400 species of fish from Heron Island coral cay. This is a greater number than from the entire North Atlantic.

We have studied the bases of the pyramid of reef life, usually called the producers; the eaters of the plants are called the consumers. Many animals are primary consumers, browsing on calcareous algae, like the parrot fish, or cropping the blue-green algae, as do various molluscs and fish.

Coral polyps are a higher level of consumers, since their stinging tentacles convert the reef into one giant "flypaper" entrapping tiny animals in the plankton. Sponges also filter out the plankton, as do bivalve molluscs such as oysters and clams. Barnacles, too, are filter feeders, straining out the plankton from the ocean waters.

Professor W. Maxwell recorded that the water volume of the Great Barrier Reef region has been estimated at 1,700 cubic miles. One fifth of this is changed each day by tidal influence.

Starfish feed on the slow-moving or fixed animals of the reef. Rays, sharks and bony fish are among the thousands of faster hunters among the consumers.

14

A third group, decomposers as they are called, feed on debris or detritus. The most obvious are the sea cucumbers, those holothurians which move over the reefs almost like earthworms shovelling in the surface sand for food particles and organic material.

In all this variety five main groups dominate the reefs—the corals, both hard and soft; the echinoderms; the molluscs; the crustaceans; and the fish.

Something has already been said of corals. There are two broad groups, the hard and the soft. The hard or true corals have tentacles grouped in multiples of six; the soft corals have these in eights. One particularly beautiful soft coral looks like a giant anemone, for it has huge leathery folds; close examination will show this is a colony of small polyps. Some polyps, on the other hand, are quite large, and mushroom corals, which are single, may grow to over a foot in diameter—but these are an exception.

Echinoderm means *spiny skinned*, and starfish, sea cucumbers, sea urchins, brittle-stars, and a few others are echinoderms. The once rare crown-of-thorns starfish has become a household word since it began to create havoc on coral reefs all over the world, to the dismay of conservationists and the astonishment of biologists. This species is a many-armed starfish, with from 13 to 17 arms, and can grow to almost two feet in diameter. The spines are poisonous which adds to the difficulty of handling it. Crown-of-thorns starfish appear to feed mainly on corals, particularly relishing the staghorn species, though some soft corals are also eaten. A fully-grown starfish can devour a square foot of coral polyps in one week. If conditions are bad it can survive without food for at least four months. Breeding occurs in a short season in midsummer, when eggs are shed into the sea. Since a female may contain up to 24,000,000 eggs and begins to breed at two years of age the opportunities for plagues to develop are obvious. These facts were gathered by a team of scientists led by Dr R. Endean, who has been in charge of the investigation into the habits of this animal. Dr Endean also found that the main predator on the crown-of-thorns is a giant mollusc known as the triton. A triton can eat one and a half starfish a week, and the removal of tritons could perhaps have been responsible for the starfish explosion. Investigations seem to show that luggers were taking about 10,000 tritons a year from the Barrier Reef.

Lying in the deeper waters of the reef are giant clams, with smaller species growing in the shallower pools. The largest known of these great molluscs measured four feet six inches in length, and the shell weighed 553 pounds. As with the other bivalves the clams are filter feeders, and two huge siphons, which suck in and later eject water, are seen as the animal feeds with its valves open. The mantle, the living tissue which secretes the shell, is often so brilliantly coloured it dims the glory of the corals near by. Like the coral polyps, clams also have a garden of algae in their flesh, and this serves the same purpose as with the corals. Recent evidence indicates that growth is rapid, and a clam reaches its three feet length within thirty years. How long it lives after that is not known.

Crustaceans belong to the same major group of organisms as insects. Just as insects are the commonest animals of the land, crustaceans are the commonest in the sea. Many live in the plankton, at least for part of their lives. Gaily coloured shrimps wander across the reef, painted crayfish lurk in coral ramparts to come out by night and feed, and even the most casual observer will at one time or another find a hermit crab. Hermit is perhaps not a suitable name, for a coral slab may have hundreds of "hermits" sheltering under it. No doubt through long association with empty shells, hermit crabs evolved to become creatures that do not need protective armour on their abdomen. However, with growth every hermit must seek a larger shell home. This may be found by searching or seized by force from another hermit.

Hermit crabs are scavengers, devouring whatever they can find. Some species have moved on to dry land, their only link with the sea coming when they need to release their larval young.

Fish are present on the reef in extraordinary variety and size, from the tiny black and white humbug to the giant Queensland groper, an unfortunate name since it is neither a groper nor confined to Queensland. Groper can be six or seven hundred pounds in weight and eight feet long.

15

Anemone fish shelter in the stinging tentacles of giant anemones, butterfly cod flaunt feather-like fins safe in their highly poisonous spines. Another less attractive creature is the stonefish, whose thirteen spines along the back can be erected when the fish is attacked. Its poison is virulent, but fortunately accidents are rare and the occasional victims recover.

There are suckerfish, where the back fin has been modified into a sucker so that the fish can hitch a ride on turtles, larger fish or boats. Flying fish scull their way out of the water and glide into the air.

Huge rays like the manta "fly" through the water with smooth undulations of the fins, and reef sharks follow reef tourists with more curiosity than evil intent. There are also larger sharks, that *are* dangerous.

These five groups are only part of the complexity and beauty of the Great Barrier Reef, the marine "eighth wonder of the world".

SURGING OCEANS *are the home of sperm whales. Cruising beyond the continental shelf at speeds of five miles an hour, the whale dives deep in search of its food, the giant squid—even to depths of three thousand feet. A male sperm whale can grow to sixty feet; the females to about half this size. Enraged bulls have been known to charge boats. At times the whales' echo-location system fails and they become stranded on sandy shores.*

Sooty terns nesting on Michaelmas Cay, North Queensland. Sea-birds range the oceans of the world, but they must come to land to nest. Tiny islands like this cay become crammed with thousands of nesting birds, and the air is filled with clamour. Food must be found within flying distance of the nesting island so that the young can be fed and the parents kept strong. Islands that fulfil these conditions are few and become highly congested. Sooty terns are found throughout all the tropical oceans of the world; they feed on small fish and other animals snipped from the surface of the ocean.

CORAL REEFS *are built by polyps that thrive in warm, clear ocean waters along the west, north and east Australian coasts. Their greatest and most spectacular growth appears in the Great Barrier Reef. A coral reef can be a few feet across, in patches or "lumps", or miles wide; it can range from highwater mark to depths of a hundred feet and more, though as the light lessens, so does the coral.*

Heron Island, a sand cay on a coral reef platform. In such formations a low, sand island is colonized by small plants. Then come larger plants, such as these pandanus trees. Even larger trees may grow, and Heron has a small pisonia forest, as well as stands of beach sheoak. The prop-like roots of the pandanus help support its trunk. The leaves are prickle-edged and in season develop large multiple fruits. These once provided food for Aborigines, who broke up and washed the seeds to make a kind of bread.

The anemone fish nestles in the stinging tentacles of a sea anemone. The poison cells of the anemone bring death to most sea dwellers; others—the anemone fish, some crabs and shrimps— are immune to this danger. They live as commensals in the protective folds of the anemone tentacles. The anemone shelters them, and they feed on scraps from the host's table.

TIDAL SEASHORES *at low tide bare, offshore reefs to heat from the sun or the chill from winter winds, and to dry air, or drenching from rain that turns salt water to fresh. Birds walk over the reefs in search of food. On the rise of the tide the whole reef world changes, with a hunt by predatory fish. At the edge of the reef, the plant and animal growth may be more vigorous, since here there is more water movement. So the rim of a reef may be slightly raised above the main reef platform.*

Not all molluscs of the seashores have protective shells. Sea hares have another device. When irritated, they exude a brightly-coloured cloud of purple. This may serve as a screen, or may be irritating to attackers. Its exact purpose is still unknown; but the shooting out of such screens by the related octopus and squid enables them to make good their escape.

On rocky shores flat rock-crabs move into crevices when danger threatens, to come out later and feed. Rock surfaces grow a coating of algae and small animal life that forms a green film. The rock crabs scrape this off for food. Fragments of larger animal life are also taken, and sometimes a fisherman finds his catch partly eaten by stealthy rock-crabs.

3
a struggle for life
TIDAL SEASHORE

One of the most fascinating habitats of all is the realm between high and low tide levels. In some places with vertical plunging cliffs this zone may be only a few feet in width. On gently sloping shores with large tidal movements as at Broome in Western Australia the zone becomes miles wide.

Some of the problems of animals and plants living in these places are obvious. If the area is sandy—soft, yielding and moving—this can clog all the functions of living with fine particles.

On rocky shores, for half of each day, at low tide, parts of the shore are exposed to air, and at high tide they are in salt water. Given a tropical downpour the salt water can become fresh. There are changes in temperature by day and night and in winter and summer. The scour of winds, and attacks by land animals and flying birds, come at low tide. With high tide marine hunters move in.

Faced with all these problems nature has a variety of solutions. Sometimes animals as different as molluscs and crustaceans take on the same device, a hard shell to protect the soft flesh.

A walk across a reef at low tide or an exploration in depth of a sandy flat, can be a scientific adventure. Australian seashores fortunately are almost entirely crown land, so access is easy. In this we are more fortunate than many other parts of the world.

The Australian mainland has about 11,300 miles of coast, with another 900 miles in Tasmania. Over this huge distance there is tremendous variation. The rocky coastlines of Tasmania, with the stronger winds from the west, have tended to create most of the big sandy beaches on the northeast. Smaller beaches can be found round the whole coastline, and these are mostly sandy with coastal dunes behind them. In Queensland the Great Barrier Reef protects the shore for 1,200 miles, so a different pattern appears with mangroves and mud flats. The Gulf of Carpentaria has sandy beaches with lagoons, salt flats and swampy areas, with mangroves in estuaries and lagoons. Northwestern Australia has immense areas of sandy flats exposed by huge tidal movements. Southwards stretch extensive sandy shores with offshore reefs, often with well-developed coral.

Coasts of South Australia, like much of southwestern Australia, have sandy bottoms with extensive growth of sea grasses. This fairly barren coastal sea is not rich in marine life, though reefs are formed to a small extent, and here a richer wildlife appears.

It would obviously be impossible to deal in more than a fragmentary way with this diversity, so a few examples are taken to show something of the life of the sandy shore and of the rocky shore.

In the sheltered areas of estuaries there is a strong growth not of seaweeds but of true land plants, the most common being the broad-leafed strapweed and the narrower eelgrass. On these meadows graze many animals from dugongs to sea hares.

17

Sea hares—molluscs which do not seem to need shells at all—come in spring and summer in huge numbers to lay their egg strands, both on sandy flats and rocky shores. They lay incredible numbers of eggs. In one season a sea hare may lay more than 400,000 and these when they hatch go to swell the plankton.

Perhaps best-known animals of the sandy shores are the burrowing pipis and beach worms. Most of the animals of this zone live buried, with "snorkels" reaching to the surface. Some burrow actively through sand, and their shapes assist in this. Being out of the light, most such animals are pale in colour and lack the splendour of the reef wildlife.

Food supplies on all shores can be listed as the plankton, already described; large algae, growing on rocks or sand; detritus—bits of plants and animals washed up on seashores; and fine material from other sources.

On these live the animals of the sandy shores. The pipi, a mollusc, is relished for food, and sought for bait. In the west a smaller species is known as the butterfly cockle; in South Australia, the pipi is known as Goolwa cockle; and Queenslanders call it the ugari. Pipis can burrow swiftly in the sand with a powerful wedge-shaped foot. Safe below the sand the pipi pushes up two long tubes called siphons. One pumps in water, loaded with oxygen, plankton and detritus; the other pumps out the used water.

This is only one of the many creatures that live in this way. Feeding on these animals are the carnivores; fish are the ones we know best, but there are others.

In the sand, too, lives the giant beach worm. This worm can grow to six feet at least, and is a devourer of debris, such as dead fish, and other marine creatures. It also actively hunts pipis and such small game.

On the reefs—rocky shores—the same pattern of food is found and the same pattern of feeding appears. Like the pipi, there are the filter feeders, which strain out detritus and plankton. Barnacles are common in such places and so are molluscs such as mussels and oysters. Barnacles are found in huge numbers; three thousand have been counted on a square foot of reef. In Sydney Harbour the masses of animals such as barnacles and oysters can be seen in well defined zones, each keeping to its own line of country.

An interesting filter feeder found at low tide on the very edge of the water is the sea squirt, known to Sydney-siders as cunjevoi. The brown bottle-shaped creatures seem like plants, but are really animals. At high tide two openings can be seen in action. Like the pipi, the cunjevoi is a filter feeder and has an entrance and exit vent. Sea squirts come both singly and in colonies. They are high on the animal "tree", starting life as tadpole-like creatures that have several features that link them with the animals with backbones. Such early promise disappears, and the sea squirt settles in one spot and grows into a bag shape.

Then there are the browsers; these work their way along the rocks, devouring algae and probably at the same time a film of animal life which lives on the surface of the seaweeds. In sandy areas of the rocky shores the browsers are absent, for there are no large seaweeds for food.

Periwinkles are the best known of the browsers, and these bluish white shellfish can be found in cracks in the reefs and on rocks which are never covered by the sea, though splashed with seawater. This splashing is enough for algae to grow, and on the algae the periwinkles feed. There are many other browsers, such as limpets which cling at low tide and move short distances at high water, cropping their own particular meadow. Sea hares can also be found browsing on some of the plants.

Then come the carnivores hunting among this mass of life. The armour of molluscs is not proof against the crushing "millstones" of the Port Jackson shark. Whelks can drill holes through the armour to feed on the soft flesh inside. Starfish, by steady pressure, force open the valves of molluscs, and Pacific gulls may pick up large shells, then rise high in the air and drop them on a rock to smash them open. Octopuses hunt crabs and other victims, and various fish move over the reefs at high tide feeding on shellfish. The succulent oyster does not have man as its only enemy. Black bream, mangrove crabs and eagle rays are some which attack it;

other enemies such as the oyster drill cut through its shell. The masses of oysters too provide a sheltering spot for a wealth of life.

Through this drama of eat and be eaten stalk the scavengers, picking up crumbs from the feeding of the carnivores. Crabs are notorious for this, and many a fisherman has found his catch attacked by rock crabs. As one British scientist said of the rock crab "it wants but little but wants that little hard".

Silver gulls are direct carnivores, but also are scavengers, the "rubbishmen" of the beaches.

4

storm-washed and drifting sands
COASTAL DUNE

People walk over beach dunes carelessly, eager for the pleasure of sea and surf. They may become more aware of dunes when the sand drifts across roads into gardens or spreads on good pasture. Some bare beach dunes are so dramatic they become spectacular landforms; some carry dense vegetation. Whether small or large, coastal dunes are never uninteresting.

Although most dunes are made of sand, some consist of fine grains of limestone—broken up coral, or shell.

The sand on the beach may be taken away by stormy weather, and built up in fine weather. Often the sand dunes lie in ridges parallel to the shore, and have been built up on beach ridges formed by the "cut and fill" action of waves.

Coastal dunes may vary from small hillocks a few feet high to the giant dunes of Queensland that rise to 924 feet on Moreton Island. These could be the highest in the world. On Fraser Island magnificent rainforest grows on dunes. Why these high dunes are found only on the Queensland coast and nowhere else in Australia is not known.

Moving from the highwater mark of spring tides there is usually a low ridge called the foredune. Behind this may be a series of moving dunes. These are slightly higher and may be separated from the foredune by a hollow. Finally comes the line of stabilized dune, which no longer moves.

In any one place the pattern may be far more complex. Perhaps a storm may have cut into the dune system. Perhaps extra sand is building out the whole beach system and a much larger area of mobile dunes is to be found. Perhaps too much use by beach buggies, grazing animals, or fire, starts the dunes moving even more and "blowouts" are formed. These are usually parabolic dunes that have made breaches in the line of parallel dunes. Trying to work out the pattern of the landforms is an interesting scientific study—as is that of the plants and animals that live on the dunes.

This is a harsh landscape. A walk over the sand in a high wind shows it. The stinging of the sand is a reminder of the abrasive effect of these grains. Well-known stories tell how Eddystone lighthouse was sandblasted, and telegraph poles cut through, by fast-moving sand grains. Most of the cutting effect is close to the ground, to a height of eighteen inches.

As well as the cutting effect of the wind there is a drying effect—taking moisture from the surface of plants or the skin of animals.

Hot summer days bring surface temperatures so high that people find it unpleasant to walk in bare feet. Winter cold produces the opposite extreme. There is also the effect of salt blown on the wind.

A sand dune may be almost pure silica with no other minerals and no humus. A plant, to succeed in such a place, must resist being torn out by the wind, and needs good anchoring roots. It must be able to prevent wind scour from damaging its leaves, and it must have devices to avoid being dried out or buried. It must be able to tolerate salt, heat and cold.

Most dune plants have well-developed root systems to help anchor them in the soil, and also to penetrate to the wet sand beneath. All early explorers knew that by digging in the depressions behind the dunes, fresh water could be found. The fresh water being less dense, floats on the saline water below. Where winter storms have cut into a dune the tremendous growth of the root systems can be seen.

The simplest way to avoid the worst effects of the wind is to cling close to the ground, and many plants do this. Wind pruning is easy to see on coastal landscapes. A mild period may allow plants to grow taller, only to be pruned back by the first wind blast.

Sheltered spots have larger and lusher plants than exposed places. Hairy leaves prevent water loss, and this is often assisted by the rolling of leaves in dry conditions. Some plants are annuals and flourish only in milder seasons, to resist as seeds the harsher times.

It would be impossible to deal with all the plants of these coastal dunes, but let us take a walk from the point of the spring high water mark, below which no land plants can survive, to the vegetated and stable dunes—a climax of which may be rainforest, heathland, gum-tree forest, or some other pattern. In between sea and climax is the plant succession. As the sand builds up or the sea retreats, the green wave of the climax moves steadily forwards overwhelming the pioneer plants.

The pioneers, by providing some stability, often lead to their own destruction, since other plants can take their place. The study of plant ecology of a coastal dune has certain fascinations. Being less complex than many others it can be studied more easily.

An interesting though puzzling feature of sand dune plants is the presence of succulents like the pigface and sea spinach. About half of the plants on sand dunes show some degree of succulence. It was often thought that this was a method by which plants could store water against their needs in dry periods. Recent evidence indicates that plants in salty soils, whether near the sea or far inland, develop this water-storing succulence because of the influence of salt on their tissues. However, the outcome may be that in times of drought they survive because of this stored water.

Many species of dune vegetation are found throughout Australia, and some are worldwide. So a traveller from Europe may feel a touch of home. The sea rocket is an excellent example. The generic name, *cakile*, comes from the Arabic *quaquillah*. The species of our shores is also found on the shores of Europe, northern Africa, and across western Asia to Australia.

Coastal dune plants are likely to drift by wind and current to a suitable habitat. When the fruits are buoyant, as with the sea rocket, thousands are washed above high-water mark by winter storms. They take root in the springtime. A few survive to grow into plants with smooth and succulent leaves. The flowers, though small, are lilac in colour, with pale green leaves. On many beaches of southern Australia the place nearest the sea is shared also by a plant known as dune arctotheca. A native of South Africa, it was found at Bunbury on the west coast in the twenties. I have seen it along the southern coastline to Jervis Bay on the east coast. The leaves and stems are fleshy with a fine white coating. The flowers are like small yellow daisies, and the plant is most attractive on the foredunes and sand flats leading to highwater mark.

In northern Australia on coral cays and sandy beaches a common creeper grows just above high-water mark—the creeping goats-foot; its leaf is divided in the shape of a cloven hoof. The large violet morning glory type flower, showy and vigorous, has long stems that run for yards over the sand.

Moving towards the less hostile foredunes various plants appear—kinds of spinifex. The name "spinifex" is also commonly used for an entirely different genus, as described for the desert dunes. The *true* spinifexes are found along the shores of Australia and Asia. Most coastal dunes have some.

At Shark Bay, on the west coast, there is a dramatic conjunction of sea spinifex and the inland "spinifex". The desert plant grows on the red desert dunes that here approach the coast. The white coastal dunes carry the green hairy spinifex and the line of demarcation is as though the spinifex had been planted by man.

Two common species on the coasts are the hairy and the long-leafed spinifex. These perennial grasses have long runners, called rhizomes, which lie buried under the sand and hold the plant well anchored. The hairy spinifex tends to anchor the foredune, and at times a sizeable hillock of sand will build up round a single plant. The long-leafed kind is more common on the mobile dunes and does not cope with the rugged conditions of the foredune so well.

The male and female of the long-leafed spinifex are on separate plants. The seeding head is large, with porcupine-like structures about ten inches in diameter. When ripe these break off and are bowled along the beach by the winds, scattering their seeds as they go. "Rolling grass" is another name for the plant, because of its travelling seed heads.

There are a number of fascinating plants on the mobile dunes, and the bibliography lists a book that gives these in some detail.

The introduced marram grass from Western Europe is now common on many coastal dunes, where it is used to stabilize the sand. There are also club rushes and sword sedges standing stiffly against the wind. The coast saltbush, a grey-leafed plant, is found only on coastal dunes throughout southern Australia. It is a plant of the mobile dunes. Here too is the prickly saltwort, also found in the desert areas. A fleshy bright green plant whose leaves glisten as though wet, the sea spinach, can be used as food, like other spinach, and one of our common species is also found in South America, New Zealand, and Japan—another example of the range of coastal plants.

One of the best known of the plants of mobile dunes, particularly in southern Australia, is the pigface. It once rejoiced in the generic name of *Mesembryanthemum*, but this has been changed to *Carpobrotus*. The native species has huge leaves like fat fingers, except that they are triangular in section. The fruits are both succulent and edible. The flowers are pink in contrast with the yellow flowers of the species introduced from South Africa.

Beyond the mobile dunes are the stable ones. Here a variety of plants may be found, until finally a climax vegetation is reached.

Wattles of various species grow, and the common species of southeastern Australia is *sophorae*. In Tasmania this is known as boobialla; the Aborigines used the seeds for food, just as the mainland Aborigines used other species of wattle. This coastal wattle is an excellent sandbinder; should branches be buried under sand, they take root and flourish. Here also the attractive coast tea-tree grows, with white flowers; the trunks twist in tortured fashion as they suffer the force of the winds. Here too are the coast banksias, from Victoria round the east coast into Queensland. The elephant grey of the bark is typical of banksia, and the yellow flower brushes appearing in winter add a touch of colour. The saw banksia grows in sandy places and forms large clumps. Historically it is interesting because it was found by Joseph Banks at Botany Bay in 1770, and bears his name. These are only a few of the interesting plants of the seashore.

There are no larger animals confined to the coastal dunes. Among the mammals, small native mice are common.

Tracks on the open sand are like the pages of a book on which, the night before, nature has written a story, sometimes prosaic, sometimes dramatic.

The dingo and fox, both introduced by man, the first by the dark Australians, the second by the white, forage along the beaches in search of flotsam. They also snap up birds sheltering from the wind in dune vegetation. One morning I found a most dramatic series of marks on a dune. From the sea came a series of web-footed tracks obviously from a pied cormorant. These went behind a spinifex clump. Then along the beach came the prints of a "dog" showing claw marks, distinguishing these from the marks left behind by feral cats, which retract their claws. Where the marks met was a confusion. Leading off to the shelter of the stable dunes was a third pattern. Here the fox pads were brushed by a dangling body while the beak scored a thin line in the sand. I followed this until in the lee of a dune I found the body of the bird with the breast eaten away.

Wallabies and, at times, grey kangaroos move to the seashore in the night, and some of these browse on the dune plants. Occasionally the tracks of an echidna may be seen—a little off its normal beat.

Birds are numerous in the dune zone. Pipits may nest in the mobile dunes, and on the fore-dunes can be found the nests of the redcapped dotterel. This dainty wader twinkles along the beach, looking for food at the water's edge. The nest is a scrape in the sand, and the chicks, once hatched, move off with their parents.

Kestrels hover, alert for grasshoppers and other insects, or perhaps a native mouse or intro-duced field mouse. Flowering plants bring hosts of honeyeaters. The singing honeyeater's melodious piping whistle is commonly heard. Seeds attract birds such as cockatoos. Roy Cooper, speaking of the coast banksia of Wilson's Promontory, said that besides its beauty, it is one of the most important food trees in the winter months.

Silver gulls forage through the coastal dunes, though most of their food is found along the water's edge and in the water itself.

Reptiles are common. Shingleback lizards are plentiful, feeding on the fleshy fruits of the dune plants, and black shiny king skinks, besides eating berries, share the scavenging habits of the shingleback. Smaller fly lizards are common darting over the sand and, at night, geckoes come from the shelter of the leaf litter in the stable dunes to forage. Small burrowing snakes like the black-striped snake are common though not often seen. Insects abound, and the characteristic "trail" of the mole cricket is most obvious. A finger run along the humped trail may find the trail-maker sheltering in a side tunnel. This cricket feeds on plant material, though it will also eat small dead animals. Its spade-shaped forelegs make admirable tunnel-ling tools. Wolf spiders run down their victims over the sand, and orb weavers spin their delicate snares between the dune bushes. Ants scurry, ever busy; and ant lions dig their pits to trap unwary ants.

The last fifty years has seen the spread of the Mediterranean land-snail, and some bushes seem white with thousands of shells. Native land-snails also occur, burying themselves deep in the sand to avoid the heat of summer, and coming out after winter showers.

Searching through the dunes at night and sometimes on overcast and cool days is the ghost crab. Insects are caught and devoured—also dead animals. In northern areas ghost crabs catch baby turtles heading for the sea. With daylight the ghost crab retreats to its burrow dug just above high water mark and reaching to the wet sand below. The crab can live in this moist home until darkness sends it out on the hunt again.

Both by day and by night coastal dunes provide a wealth of natural interest.

5
rich mud and ooze
MANGROVE FOREST

For a traveller shipwrecked on a lonely coast a mangrove forest can be a terror-filled place of ooze, of slippery roots, and an agonizing struggle through a labyrinth that seems to have no pattern and no end, with crocodiles a lurking menace and bloodsucking mosquitoes and midges a persistent irritation.

Yet for a naturalist well coated with insect repellent and with time to watch, there can be few places more packed with lively interest.

Mangrove forests are found throughout the world, mostly in the tropics but penetrating into temperate regions. Some mangroves are found along the southern coastline of Victoria, South Australia, and Western Australia—perhaps a reminder that the whole of Australia was once a lusher continent than the arid land it is today.

Salt water and mangroves go together. These forests grow only where, at some time, perhaps every day, but at least at spring tides, their root systems are submerged by the sea. The trees grow in muddy flats in the zone between land and sea. This may be on an exposed coastline as at Broome, or in sheltered estuaries many miles from the sea in places along the eastern and northern coastline. The stronghold of these forests is the Queensland coast, where they grow vigorously in the rich ooze washed down by coastal rivers. Far out to sea on coral cays, and on the islands of the Abrolhos, mangroves also flourish, often on coral mud. Where vigorous wave action removes the mud as fast as it is poured into the sea, no mangroves can take hold.

Most trees of the mangroves favour the tropics. Dr Len Webb lists these species as we travel southward: Northern Australia, 27; Cairns, 24; Proserpine, 22; Moreton Bay, 10; northern N.S.W., 4; Sydney, 2; and southern Australia, only one.

Not all trees in the mangrove are closely related, but all do share the ability to thrive in the transition zone of land and sea. Salt water regularly flushes their root systems, yet they must be able to survive with roots buried under fresh water at flood-time. Because of the regular washing by tides, many mangroves have acquired what is called *viviparity*. In such plants the seeds develop on the tree in normal fashion and then actually germinate on the mother tree. Some grow shoots up to a foot long, so when they drop to the mud below they have already a start in life, compared with seeds of dry land trees that fall to the ground and then must germinate and grow.

The muddy, salty, mangrove world has produced various adaptations. Salt water destroys normal plants by drawing the water out of their tissues and drying them out. Trees of the mangrove counter this drying out in several ways. They have the typical mangrove leathery leaf, sometimes glossy and sometimes dull; the sap is adapted to resist the pull of the salt water outside; in some still unknown way many have tannins that assist. The lack of air in the mud where the roots grow is overcome by breathing stems called pneumatophores, that rise from the mud round the knee roots of some species, or round prop roots that run out "flying buttresses"; or, most extraordinary of all, there are mangroves that push out thousands of "fingers" into the air, aerial roots that allow the plant to breathe. Roots as well as leaves must have oxygen.

Although mangrove forests are not known for giant trees, some up to 125 feet are found in the tropics. Australian forests are smaller, and on windswept coastal islands the trees may be no more than three or four feet high. Even so, the trunks are often large and make up for their lack of height by twisting over the mud parallel to the ground.

The most extraordinary feature of a mangrove forest is the apparent lack of small plants. We are used to seeing many ground cover plants below a tree canopy—small trees, shrubs, grasses and a host of other plants. In mangroves, at first glance, there are trees and nothing else; but to the eye of the botanist there are highly characteristic algae or seaweeds that grow in roots or other places above the mud level. Where remains of shells or stones lie on the forest floor, other larger algae may flourish. In the ooze grow the microscopic forms of plant life that make up most of the pastures of the sea.

Landward of the mangroves there may be swards of glasswort, a *Salicornia*; then rushes and some grass, then stunted sheoaks, and finally forest. Seaward, with a little more sand mixed with the mud, there may be swards of land plants that have adapted themselves to the sea. Best known is the eelgrass, *Zostera*, and the strapweed, *Posidonia*.

An acre of sea is usually much richer in its animal production than an acre of dry land. In speaking of desolate areas of marine marsh and mangrove swamp, Dr G. G. T. Harrison, Chief Inspector of Fisheries and Senior Biologist of the Department of Harbours and Marine in Queensland, has explained that the intricate root system of the mangrove holds the mud firm. If not held in estuaries and bays the mud will travel on, perhaps blocking navigable rivers and harbours. As fresh water flows or seeps through the mud it picks up nutrients, some from normal run-off from the land, some from decaying leaves. This water runs into the shallows and helps in the growth of algae and other plants of the sea. Dr Harrison goes on to say: "Mangrove forest shores, mudflats and associated marine grass beds are the natural habitat of a number of aquatic organisms of economic importance. Some of these organisms occupy the habitat in adult phase, some in juvenile phase and some throughout life. These coastal marshes are among the most naturally fertile areas in the world and experimental evidence has demonstrated a rate of production of basic food materials in the range of 60 to 240 pounds per acre per day. These production rates are difficult to rival even under the best conditions of modern horticulture with artificial fertilisers. This is the food which supports the fishes and crustaceans of the region during those parts of their lifetimes when they are in the inshore waters".

Dr Harrison worked out the value of such "useless" marine marshes in their feeding of oysters, prawns, fish at $300 an acre a year.

In Indonesia mangroves are cut for firewood and the ponds so created used for culturing fish and prawns. As a result they bring a return in terms of animal protein higher than the best agricultural land. The Chinese extract tannin from mangroves, and figures from Hainan Island show that every two and a half acres return in money as much as one acre of first class rice-field. This is in addition to the animal life the mangroves nourish.

As with the other habitats only a small part of the animal life can be spoken of here. Mammals are few, though various kinds of rats scavenge. Mangrove and rainforest are favoured camps of the fruit bats, safe from human attack, for a retreat deep in a huge area of mangrove is not easy for people to reach.

Birds of the mangrove are legion. Some are closely linked with the habitat, as their names show—mangrove heron, mangrove kingfisher, mangrove robin. Keith Hindwood in a study of birds in mangroves near Sydney lists 104 different species, some introduced, and of these 39 nest in the area. He lists the following as typically mangrove-haunting: great-billed heron, mangrove and yellow-billed kingfisher, mangrove heron, mangrove robin, brown whistler, white breasted whistler, broadbilled flycatcher, mangrove warbler, and mangrove honeyeater.

Chestnut teal may be found in mangrove streams, and near Sydney there once appeared a colony of nankeen night herons. Sea eagles, herons, darters, cormorants and other fish-eaters find mangroves an ideal home.

Two groups of reptiles are outstanding in the mangrove. Most fearsome are the saltwater or estuarine crocodiles. The mangrove waterways make an ideal living place for them. The record length for a crocodile in Australia is 32 feet, and 25-foot crocodiles were once common. Intense hunting has destroyed most of the larger animals, and in many places they were harried to extinction. Once they were found from Broome on the west coast, along the whole of northern Australia, south to the Tropic of Capricorn on the east coast. Their food varies from tadpoles and fish when young, to mud crabs, fish and turtles, and small and large mammals. Nesting takes place in sandbanks above high-tide mark, close to mangrove creeks. The nest is a kind of compost heap where the eggs are hatched by the warmth of decaying leaves. The mother crocodile guards the nest against enemies that would eat the eggs or newly emerged young.

Common lizards that feast on crocodile eggs, birds, crabs and fish are the mangrove monitor and the water goanna. The water goanna has its tail flattened like that of the crocodile to help in swimming. It also has the typical nostril and eye profile of the crocodile, which allows the animal to lie in the water mostly submerged yet still able to see and breathe.

Among the insects, the best known are the mosquitoes, and the so-called sandflies, which could more accurately be called biting midges. Tidal pools left behind by spring tides provide breeding grounds for mosquitoes, which can breed in salt water. More research is needed to show the life histories of other insects, and because of their importance to man this is now being carried out.

Spiders feed richly on the profusion of insects, as do some of the smaller insect-eating birds. Woodswallows are therefore common in mangrove creeks.

Among the inhabitants of the water and mud we find spectacular animals. Of the fish, none attracts as much attention as the tree-climbing mud-skipper. Some mud-skippers feed by scraping plant life off the mud, others hunt small prey. Some even climb the mangrove roots in search of insects. Though breathing by gills, they can stay out of water for many minutes. The gill covers bulge out, and no doubt the air trapped inside in contact with the moist gills enables the fish to live. It is said that these fish can also breathe through the skin near the tail in much the same way as does a frog, taking dissolved oxygen out of the water directly. It is fascinating to see them skipping nimbly over the mud, and sometimes hopping in kangaroo fashion. Others merely slither over the mud like eels. Some species are able to raise bright-coloured fins in display, and these are prized for saltwater aquariums. The display of such fish can be spectacular as the male leads the females to the mud saucers used as breeding pools. Some species build turrets of mud, and they lie with their pectoral fins resting on the crater edge. As befits a land-hunting creature the eyes can be swivelled to search for prey or danger. Of more interest to fishermen are fish like the mullet, common in mangrove streams; and in Queensland the much relished fish called the mangrove jack (a large one can reach 25 pounds, but an angler must be alert, for the hooked fish dart for cover among the mangrove roots).

Crustaceans are common, but only a few kinds will be described. The mud crab can grow to nine inches across the carapace, and is delicious eating. One way to hunt the crab is to search through the mangroves at low tide and probe the deep tunnels with a long iron hook. This crab is found round coastlines washed by the Indian Ocean, and on the Pacific coastline of Australia and northwards to China.

The mud crab is a sombre-coloured swimming crustacean, but the smaller fiddler crabs are among the most gaily patterned of all the mangrove creatures. Depending on the location, on exposure to sun, and on the kind of silt, many kinds of fiddlers can be found along the mangrove shores. Some are brilliant scarlet, some sky blue, some yellow, and some mixed in colour.

The female has two small claws. She feeds by picking up fragments of mud, then sifting this of edible material by means of hairs in the adjacent two legs. Since the strainers on these legs can handle a certain size of soil particles only, the different species of fiddler crabs space themselves neatly in various areas of the mud. The male, though feeding in similar fashion, has one claw enlarged so that it is as long and broad as the rest of the body.

If you wander over the mangrove flats at low tide the crabs disappear into their burrows. After a few moments of immobile waiting you will see them come out and feed once more. The large claw of the male is useful for holding territory. Occasionally you can see a male pursuing another male to its burrow and perhaps poking a tentative claw after its opponent. The great claw is used also as part of a courtship dance, brandished like a gaudy cloak, and sometimes stretched in beckoning fashion. In some species dance steps may be added as an extra attraction.

Equally gaily coloured though lacking the large claw of the fiddlers are the soldier crabs. These globular crabs march along the mud at low tide in formation, though when attacked the regiments of crabs melt into the mud, each burrowing in spiral fashion.

Three kinds of these soldier crabs are found in Australia, with one species or another on west and east coasts, and round northern Australia. As with the fiddlers, food is gained from the mud, and when the soil has been strained of its food particles washed in by the previous tide, the mud is discarded as little pellets. Thousands of such pellets are an indication of the crab army, even though the animals themselves may have moved a hundred yards farther on.

Then there are the mud lobsters. A small kind, pale in colour, is found along the eastern Australian coasts, and is known as the yabbie; it lives in burrows in the sandy mud. Fishermen capture yabbies by placing a simple sucking pump over the feeding holes, the entrance to the burrows, and drawing them into the tube of the pump.

There is another much larger mud lobster found from northern Australia, south to central Queensland. This crustacean can grow to about ten inches long, and is usually shades of red and yellow.

Mud lobsters live in burrows and feed mainly by night, though on rainy days they feed freely—even at times in full sunlight. Though well armoured, they are remarkably clumsy, climbing with difficulty and feeding in the mud of pools left behind by the receding tide.

Molluscs are common in mangrove areas. Best known is the rock oyster. The first settlers soon noted the clusters of oysters growing in Sydney Harbour. In the words of Surgeon Arthur Bowes, writing in 1788; ". . . all the rocks near the water are thick covered with oysters, which are very small but finely flavoured; they also adhere to the branches of the mangrove trees".

Since early in the oyster's life it changes from a free-floating existence to settle on a hard surface, the spat, as it is called, finds its way to mangrove branches, trunk or roots. Oyster farmers for many years used black mangrove sticks, chosen because the bark was smooth and would allow the oysters to be peeled off with the bark. Also marine borers such as the teredo tend not to attack mangrove wood. The rock oyster needs three years to reach maturity.

A glance at the oysters will show that they cluster at levels where conditions favour them. Also, you may see by collecting oysters from different localities that they tend to grow where the water is less saline. Their growth is also affected by the amount of food, and competition from other oysters. So the final shape and size of an oyster shell depends on many things.

Other molluscs, like the Hercules club shell, can be seen crawling on the muddy flats, and smaller periwinkles may be found in the mangrove branches.

These are only a small part of the animal life of a mangrove. There is here a lifetime of study.

6
wildflower gardens
HEATHLAND

"A wasteland covered with small shrubs" is the dictionary definition of a heath. The word is an old English one, so a heath is not something purely Australian—but here the heathlands present some remarkable features.

Heaths of one kind or another are found over most of the country, on the coasts north of Geraldton in Western Australia, in the southwest regions, and along the coastlines to eastern Australia and Tasmania, then northwards into Queensland. Usually heathlands are thought of as areas covered with low shrubs, many showing the typical "heathy" leaf—short and sharp-pointed, only a few reaching a height of about five feet. However, there is also country called "tree-heath", where scattered small trees grow. In Southern Australia these trees are usually mallees, but elsewhere banksia and other single-trunked trees. In most heaths, the shrubs grow close packed, in some more open.

The low habit of growth in good rainfall areas means low soil fertility. Normally the heaths grow on sandy soils where over many years the mineral salts have been leached out of the soil. The growing layer for the plants is almost pure sand, lacking phosphates and nitrogen. Heath plants overcome this disadvantage by holding and using the little phosphorus available. Fungal threads growing in close association with the roots act as root hairs, which are able to tap large amounts of soil and pass the benefit to their host plants. Bushfires can sweep over heath country and do little damage. The plants grow fresh shoots from the root stocks that have remained unharmed in the soil.

Poverty of soil and the ability of the native plants to thrive while the introduced grasses could not gain a foothold kept the heathlands of Australia safe from development until the last twenty years or so. It was a challenge to the agricultural scientists to solve the problem so that this land could be used by man. The native plants were growing at rates that compared quite favourably with crops on good soils near by.

In these heathland communities there is a tremendous variety of plants. A Government Botanist of Western Australia, C. A. Gardner, put it this way: "The flora of Western Australia exhibits its greatest diversity, its greatest numbers, and its most interesting and colourful endemic species in the sand heath formations, which are one of the best 'gardens' of the State's famous wildflowers."

It is no wonder that the botanists have treasured such places and look with alarm at modern developments that are destroying these "treasure chests" not yet unlocked.

It was discovered that by adding superphosphate and various trace elements the former "wastelands" could be used for grazing. Millions of acres have been converted in the last twenty years, and it is important that throughout Australia adequate reserves of heathland are set up.

In Western Australia heath grows wherever there is deep sand. At times this may grade into gravelly sands. Often dwarf trees grow, particularly mallees, banksias and grass trees. On the

28

coast there is much heathland, and large reserves have been set up from Geraldton north to the Murchison River. The coastal heath country between Esperance and Israelite Bay also has its reserve. Inland, beyond the forests more sand heath country opens out, locally called "sandplain". This extends to the arid country inland, though the numbers of plant species drop as the country becomes drier.

In South Australia areas of "light land" such as the Coonalpyn Downs have sandy country with strong development of heaths, and heath is also merged with extensive areas of mallee.

In Victoria heaths develop on the coast and also around the Grampians, with extensions into the mallee.

Tasmania has coastal heaths in the northwest, northeast and on other narrow parts of the coast, as well as on the Bass Strait islands.

New South Wales has heaths and tree heaths along the coast. These extend well into Queensland. (The word *wallum* is used for a kind of heath—with some variations. Dr F. W. Whitehouse describes wallum: ". . . a special kind of heath country in which the sands are not derived from local rocks but from the denudations of great sandhills of Pleistocene age".)

For many people "heath" is an Erica, a garden plant brought from Europe and planted in Australian gardens. Because of similarity of conditions, introduced heath and native heath look very much alike, but the Australian group belong to the Epacrids. This is a family found only in the southern hemisphere, mainly in Australia, New Zealand, New Caledonia and sub-Antarctic islands. At first glance the flowers, leaves and habit of growth are very similar.

The best known of the southern varieties is the common heath, found in Victoria, South Australia and north to the central areas of New South Wales. Normally pink, blooms can vary from white through pink to scarlet. Those found in the Grampians are noted for handsome pink bells. Other heath plants are the beard heaths—among them the sea currant, whose white fruit is much relished by lizards, birds, possums, and people who make it into jam. There are also the fuschia heaths, the Astrolomas, and the extraordinary Richeas, the best known of which is the huge Pandanni of Tasmania. Here the heath plant grows as a large "tree" perhaps twenty feet in height and looking more like a palm than a heath.

Not only plants belonging to the Epacrids grow in heathlands. There can be orchids, acacias, gum-trees, banksias and grass-trees.

Among the great diversity of plants live many kinds of animals—though these of course are limited by the overall nature of the vegetation. Food, shelter and a place to raise young are essential to any animal. One would not expect to see koalas in tree-less areas. As a general rule, because of the lack of cover, most of the animals of heathlands are small, though at times larger creatures such as emus and kangaroos may move across heaths to reach a feeding ground.

Overhead, eagles and smaller birds of prey quarter the ground in search of victims.

Mammals are not numerous and are mostly small. Echidnas forage for termites, and honey possums compete with the honeyeating birds for nectar from flowers. The small pygmy possums have a diet of insects and nectar. On the ground bandicoots dig for grubs, and fat-tailed dunnarts take insects or, in the cold of winter, lie coiled up in a dead grass-tree stump. Bush rats, the eastern swamprats, and the grey mouse, are the rodents most common in heathland areas.

Cayley's *What Bird Is That*? devotes a large section to birds of the heath and undergrowth. Small birds including scrub-wrens, emu-wrens, field-wrens, grass-wrens, finches and fairy wren are seen. Honeyeaters, flock here in the flowering season. The tawnycrowned honeyeater is a heathland honeyeater, a bird typical of the habitat. The brush bronzewing pigeon is another bird of the heathlands, though not only found here, and so also is the ground parrot.

J. Forshaw, in his book *Australian Parrots*, in commenting on the parrots he studied at the Barren Grounds Nature Reserve in New South Wales, remarked on the fact that when heaths are protected from fires, the plants grow tall and dense and the parrots disappear. After fires, when the heath begins to grow once more, the parrots reappear. Ideal conditions arise about three years after burning, then last for another three to four years. So, proper management of a heathland needs a "mosaic" burning, so that a wide variety of growth patterns will develop and wildlife can flourish. This is the kind of basic research needed for all our habitats.

Insects are common and most orders are represented. Where there are insects there are spiders. The beautiful spiny spiders are often called Christmas spiders by children because of the brightness of their colouring. At times, webs of gossamer spread over the low shrubbery. Jewel beetles and butterflies sip at the nectar. At night, moths and other insects tap this flow and, both in the air and on the ground, birds and mammals take their honey at second hand by eating the nectar feeders. An engrossing study is to watch the flowering spike of a grass-tree by day and by night. I once saw a boobook owl on a bent flowering spike pick off insects as they came to feed.

The wildlife of the heaths is interesting but not obvious. Yet many people get delight from the sight of bright birds drinking at even brighter flowers. For the scientist, this treasure house will release gems of knowledge for years to come.

7
a disappearing asset
FRESHWATER LAKE

Lakes can be formed in many ways. There are those formed by a warping of the earth's surface to make a hollow where water can collect. A number of lakes appear to have taken shape in this way—such as the Great Lake in Tasmania and lakes Buchanan and Galilee in Queensland. Some lakes are formed by glacial action. Tasmania has many of these. Four thousand occur in the northwestern section of the Central Plateau.

There are also volcanic crater lakes, such as the Blue Lake of Mt Gambier and the well-known lakes Barrine and Eacham on the Atherton Tableland.

Billabongs formed by rivers flooding over their banks are another type. Some are formed when wind erodes and scoops hollows in the earth; landslides can dam rivers; chemical solution of rocks may form hollows that become lakes; sand barriers formed by wind can act as dams. Near the coastlines such dune lakes are common. Although sand is porous, gradually humus accumulates in such hollows. Finally chemical action cements sand grains into an impermeable bedrock. Some of these dune lakes may be well above sea-level as with the Boomerang Lakes on Fraser Island, four hundred feet above the sea. Dr E. A. E. Bayly in discussing the coastal lakes of Queensland points out how such "perched" lakes are very vulnerable, since any damage to the basin bedrock will mean that the lakes drain away. The same danger faces dune lakes elsewhere.

Often the water of these lakes is brown, from the humus material dissolved in it. Brown water is acid, and a lack of lime affects the plants and animals living there. While these dune lakes are mostly permanent with some fluctuations in water level with the season, the farther inland one travels, the greater the changes in the lake systems and the kinds of salts they contain. Many become more and more brackish till finally the salt level becomes higher than that of the sea.

Some are ephemeral, lasting only a few months. Others may linger for years, then slowly dry out. Lake George (a large area of water) near Canberra, is an example. Its basin was apparently formed by faulting in the slates of the area. When rainfall is high, the lake fills, but drought years evaporate the water until the lake dries out. Records give its vicissitudes—a lake from 1816 to 1830, then dry except for some slight fillings; in 1874 it filled and stayed full till 1900. Accurate records have not been kept, but it was mostly dry for a long period, till 1959; then it filled again. It is still full today, though falling.

Whatever the original formation of a lake, it will gradually shallow from silt washed in, decaying animal and plant life, and dust and debris from the air. Its fate is to move inexorably to a climax—to become dry land, unless a sinking of the basin keeps rejuvenating it. In a country as arid as Australia great fluctuations in water depths occur. In southwest Australia 67% of all the wetlands disappear in the summer dry and return with the winter rains. As a result the plants and animals have evolved to take advantage of the various stages of evaporation and replenishment.

Some of the plants of these freshwater habitats have already been discussed in the section on rivers, but the still waters of swamps and lakes allow a greater growth of plant life. Some plants are able to thrive both in water and on the wet mud when the water evaporates. Seeds lying in the dried mud can have a long life. The sacred lotus has seeds that appear to be able to survive for at least 2,000 years.

The plants of the lakes can be grouped roughly as those that float free and those rooted in the bottom. Along the edges, the water-loving plants are replaced by shrubs and trees. As time gradually converts the lake into dry land, the plants growing round the edges march forward in a green wave to overwhelm those of the open water.

Among the most interesting of the free-floating forms are the duckweeds—the smallest of all flowering plants. *Wolffia* is the smallest genus and *Lemna*, slightly larger, is better known. Most new plants are produced by budding off from the parent. Soon duckweed spreads rapidly like green confetti on the water.

Another common floating plant forms a red carpet on the surface—the red azolla fern. As with the duckweed new plants are produced by budding.

Best known of all the floating plants is the water hyacinth, brought from tropical America as an ornamental plant. In the colder southern States it has not proved a problem; but in warmer areas it spreads rapidly over still water, and a single plant has been known to cover 700 square yards in one season of growth. With swollen green leaves, filled with air and very buoyant, the floating mass becomes a solid barrier to boat transport and water movement. In several States it has been declared a noxious weed. The mauve flowers are beautiful and the plants a haven for water animals. Goldfish owners find hyacinth useful in ponds; the roots provide a sheltered place for the eggs.

In earlier days the hyacinth was dragged ashore and used as compost. A "cheaper" method of getting rid of it is to use chemical spray. In the long run this may be more expensive, since the rotting hyacinth forms a rich layer for the growth of midge larvae and adds to the silting up of the lake.

Among the plants rooted to the bottom there are the water milfoils, with their vigorous growth, familiar in most parts of the world. Inland there is the nardoo, a fern that produces spore cases valued as a source of flour by the Aborigines in earlier times, and known in the Burke and Wills story. There are also water lilies, the yellow swamp lily of the southern lakes and various kinds in warmer waters. Most beautiful of all is the sacred lotus, found from the Middle East, through India and Asia to northern Australia. The Aborigines find gastronomic, as well as visual delight in the lotus; they eat its tubers and seeds. The hollow-leaf stalks once served as snorkels to move under water in pursuit of prey or when escaping from enemies.

Another plant of shallow waters, the bulrush, grows in many parts of the world. Smaller are the various sedges, spike rushes and water ribbons.

There are also the delightful fairies' aprons, or utricularia, a dainty flower on a blood-thirsty plant. It grows in shallow water and has specially modified leaves as trapping bladders to catch small animal victims by drawing them in with a rush of water.

A study starting from the middle of a pond and moving to dry land is a fascinating one, showing how plants change to suit their habitat. A similar study over a number of years, during winter and summer, wet and dry, and the slow change produced by time, can be even more fascinating.

The animals of such areas are diverse. A high-power microscope reveals a new world in a drop of pond water or a sample of slime from the bottom. Amoeba, a plant well known to all biology students, can be found here. There are also tiny octopus-like animals, the hydra, whose marine relatives are corals and anemones. Red bloodworms squirm in the mud, and as adults will make up the swarms of midges that dance over the water on still evenings. Wrigglers writhe through the water as larvae, or tumble as pupae, to emerge finally as blood-sucking mosquitoes. Stalking through the underwater jungles are the larvae of dragonflies, which devour wrigglers.

COASTAL DUNES, *with their plant zones as seen from highwater mark. Closest to the water are the sea rockets. On the fore-dune grows creeping spinifex. On the hind dunes, where weather conditions are less severe, bigger shrubs take over, dominated by tea-trees. Even so, all the taller shrubs are pruned by sea winds, and the plants slope upwards until, in full shelter, they can grow to a greater height.*

In the tropics, coastal dunes become the home of "goat's-foot creeper", sometimes called "beach morning glory". Both the drying effect of moving air, and the salt the air contains, can damage plant life; and there is also the scour caused by sand grains lifted by the wind. Most plant colonizers creep close to the ground, and a strongly developed root system not only taps the water supply held in the sand, but also anchors the plant.

MANGROVE FOREST *on the Abrolhos Island. Mangroves are found right round the Australian mainland. Growing on sheltered mud flats, they have an unusual root system to handle this environment. In their cover live many animals—crabs, fish, birds. This young sea eagle was hatched in a nest built in a tree near by, and waits on the edge of a mud pool for its parents to bring food—a young noddy tern taken from a nest in the mangrove.*

Where river-mouths broaden as they reach the sea, wide expanses of sand and water appear. Tides affect plant and animal life—both at the mouth and well upstream. This estuary in Tasmania shows a pattern of sand dunes, shallow and deep water lagoons, and the sea beyond. At times estuaries may be muddy and fringed with mangroves. The edges of estuaries are held firm by glassworts and marine rushes, and the shallow water develops rich flats of sea grasses.

HEATHLAND, *on a road edge. Western Australia has become known as the wildflower State. Grevilleas, feather flowers and smokebush bring splashes of colour. The heathlands carry many of the three thousand species of wildflowers found in the southwest corner. About three-quarters of these are found nowhere else. Though the particular flowers may be small, they are often grouped so closely together that the effect is striking.*

This eucalyptus flower, mottlecah, sometimes known as rose of the west, is found only in the southwest corner. Eucalyptus means "well covered" and refers to the cap that protects the bud and falls away when the flower develops. The mottlecah flower may be over two inches in diameter, the largest known among eucalypts. The plant is now widely grown as an ornamental shrub.

This lizard, known by many names—bobtail, shingleback, sleepy—has a bright blue tongue which, when displayed against a wide open pink mouth, frightens off most attackers. The lizard belongs to the skink family and, like all Australian lizards, is harmless. Its food consists of vegetation such as fungi, flowers, fruit, and at times small animals dead or alive. Common in the heathland, it is also found in a wide variety of habitats.

FRESHWATER LAKES. *Much of Australia was once covered with lakes, some permanent, some disappearing in the dry season. Most of the coastal lakes in southern States have been drained, often in shortsighted "conservation" work; but many inland and tropical ones remain. This Northern Territory swamp, in the dry season, attracts many birds such as herons, magpie geese and jabirus. In the wet these will nest in vegetation that then appears in the lakes.*

Among the crustaceans are the best known of freshwater animals. Just as sandhoppers feed on decaying seaweeds, there are freshwater animals that feed on the weed. The water-flea, or daphnia, jerks its way through the water. Daphnia appear as if by magic, even in the smallest pools, having survived as eggs in dry periods. In various water-works all over the country, daphnia are busily engaged in grazing water plants, and so prevent these becoming a problem. Even then, filters in such works often remove daphnia in tons.

There are also the larger freshwater crayfishes—yabbies, jilgies, koonacs, the giant marron of the south west, and the Murray River crayfish. Tasmania has a giant that reaches eight pounds in weight. Large or small—all are delightful food and provide enjoyment in the catching. Some burrowing species can be a problem, by damaging banks of dams and so releasing water.

From a scientific point of view the "living fossils" of Tasmania, the mountain shrimp *Anaspides* is most famous. Unlike true shrimps the body is straight and the front half has segments instead of a solid carapace.

A less pleasant animal of pools and moist forests is the bloodsucking leech—a kind of worm related to the earthworm. There are various kinds of leeches.

Fish are numerous in the deeper pools, such as the introduced mosquito fish or gambusia, and the goldfish or other carp. The European carp has become a pest species because of its habit of stirring up mud while feeding.

Frogs delight in pools, and there are various kinds. Burrowing frogs dig their burrows in stream banks. The eggs may be laid here in the typical frothy mass. Development proceeds so that when rains cause a rise in water level to flood the burrow, the tadpoles have a good start in life.

From frogs to ducks is a natural step. Dr H. Frith has found an interesting pattern between water levels and duck breeding. Musk ducks and the related bluebill ducks need deep permanent pools for feeding and breeding. Some birds, like the wood-duck, are grazers, and when food is plentiful breed along the edges of swamps. The common grey teal starts to breed as soon as the first rains come. Eggs were found in a teal ten days after rain had fallen. A little later than the teal, in taking advantage of the water, are the black duck.

The hardheads need deep pools. The beautiful little pink-eared ducks, which feed on plankton, breed in the last phases of flooding when huge areas of shallow water lead to a good development of food in pools that are gradually decreasing.

In the north the magpie goose begins to nest in the later stages of the summer wet. Among the other waterbirds are grazers such as coots and native hens; hunters of small fish, frogs and yabbies, like the whitefaced herons; and spoonbills, which sift the mud with splayed bills.

Also hunting the water for small fry are freshwater tortoises, and in northern pools freshwater crocodiles join in the chase.

Mammals are not as common as other groups, yet all over Australia the water rat can be found; its beautiful fur and whitetipped tail are good identification marks. For water rats, mussels provide staple food; but they are also snappers up of various "trifles".

The introduced water buffalo has taken with relish to the pools in the Northern Territory, and has stripped many of these of their native vegetation, for buffaloes are active feeders in freshwater areas both in and out of the water. No doubt the coating of thick mud from their wallows offers protection against attacks of bloodsucking insects.

It is tragic that many fascinating wetlands of Australia have been largely destroyed, often for unwise drainage projects that have turned valuable wildlife areas into poor farmland.

8
the green wave
ROCK SUCCESSION

First there was rock. The story of the land starts on bare rock. Here life struggles for a foothold. Any rock can be studied to see this drama of life; but the more even-grained outcrops such as granite, limestone and sandstone offer the best surfaces.

The first life on the bare surface could be bacteria; but the next stage, the invasion by algae, is more obvious. The black surface seen on outcrops comes with such plants. Algae accelerate the work of breaking the hard surface, adding to the shattering effect of heat and cold, and the chemical destruction by water. Once the surface is sufficiently pitted, the lichens move in. Lichens are an unusual partnership between fungi and algae. Crustose lichens are common and some species are colourful, making a boulder a study in browns, yellows and reds.

Slowly a thin film of soil begins to accumulate from the decay of lichens, the trapping of dust, as well as particles from the breaking of the rock surface. A green sward of moss takes hold. This retains even more water under its surface, which together with increasing soil depth allows other plants to establish themselves. Larger lichens begin to grow; and needle-bush, a species of Borya; sundews and orchids; as well as rock ferns and the pioneer higher forms of plants. As the years pass the soil cover thickens until it may be several inches deep. Often joints in the original rock become enlarged and form deeper crevices, where there is enough soil to allow the roots of large plants to grip and draw water and mineral salts. In the main these plants will be found also in the near-by forest; but they will be more prevalent on the shallow soils of the rock than elsewhere. Native geraniums, needle-bushes, darwinias and the like are common. In the more shaded cracks ferns are prolific. Here too will grow various orchids such as the helmet and the greenhood, together with other water-loving plants.

The soil deepens over the passing years, and larger shrubs appear. Slowly the rock crumbles as plant succeeds plant. At last, like a green wave, the surrounding forest or other plant association moves in as the climax of the succession.

The animals of these successions on rocks are not so obvious as the plants. With the first plants also comes microscopic animal life such as protozoans. Larger creatures such as millipedes, centipedes, and spiders move in with the increasing amount of vegetation and soil. These small animals are similar to those found in near-by areas. Under slabs of rock an interesting series of animals live. Flat huntsman spiders are common, and slide in sideways under new crevices should a slab be lifted. Here, also, shelter numerous reptiles, such as barking lizards and velvet geckoes. Dragon lizards run swiftly over the rocks in search of food.

For the reptiles the cold of winter may mean a period of hibernation. Sunny days can bring activity. A warming up period in the sun is necessary before hunting begins. In summer the reverse holds true, hunting in the sunshine alternating with cooling-off periods in the shade. For the geckoes, activity can take place at a much lower body temperature than for the dragons.

A West Australian scientist, S. D. Bradshaw, recently studied the ornate dragon, a small lizard found in Western Australia. Many desert animals fight the heat and lack of water by changing their behaviour patterns, but some survive by physiological changes. In the ornate dragon some of the babies grow much faster than the others. The bigger youngsters survive better in frosty winters. When summer droughts come those of the smaller lizards that have managed to survive the cold of winter are able to last better without water. So the "swing" of the winter is balanced by the "roundabout" of summer.

In time, with action of plant and animal, wind and rain, the rock disappears, engulfed by the green wave of plant-life.

9
the blue mirage
SALT LAKE

The blue lake areas on maps of inland Australia may mislead visitors into thinking this a well-watered country. Such lakes may be dry in most years, and if filled with water, may be salt.

Salt lakes are an important habitat, and vary from a few acres of valley floor to the huge Lake Eyre Basin. This lake covers about 3,000 square miles, and drains a half million square miles of country in South Australia, New South Wales, and Queensland.

The salt in the soils and lakes of Australia comes partly from the rock itself or from soils drained by rivers that feed the lake, and partly from the air. Two hundred miles east of Perth it was found that, with the rain each year, also came sixteen pounds of salt to the acre.

Many lakes have formed through old drainage systems becoming sluggish, either by tilting of the land as with Lake Eyre, or by drying out in an arid period some thousands of years ago.

With the clearing for farms of the deeprooted plants, which act as water pumps, the groundwater rose. Since in many places this water was salt, once good soil became a salt-pan. All these factors combined in the formation and steady increase of salt lakes.

The sodium chloride in the lake water may be at concentrations several times saltier than the sea. The waters are clear, since the colloidal clay that keeps fresh waters muddy for long periods is precipitated by the action of the salt.

Gypsum is another mineral commonly found in salt lakes; and on lake shores accumulations can occur, in dunes, of material known as kopai.

Froth forms when winds stir up waves on salt lakes. The lines of foam are a feature of most of these lakes. Because the floors of so many salt lakes are almost flat, wind tides occur as the water migrates back and forth, depending on the direction of the wind. Speeds of two inches a second are common, and the animals in the water are carried along with the wind tides.

The life includes organic debris, some microscopic plant plankton, and the animals that feed on them. There are fly larvae, caddis flies, and numerous crustaceans. Best known are the brine shrimps, close relatives of the fairy shrimps of freshwater lakes. Although separately very difficult to see because of their transparent appearance, at times tens of thousands gather in swarms about the size of a football—and then become obvious. As with the other dwellers in ephemeral pools, many eggs are laid to keep the race alive during the dry. Brine shrimp eggs are gathered in huge amounts in other parts of the world for aquarists, who find the eggs and the freshly hatched larvae excellent food for aquarium animals.

The banded stilt, a long-legged wading bird, seems to depend on an abundance of the brine shrimp for successful breeding. At times colonies of several thousand birds may be found nesting when heavy rain creates good conditions in salt lakes. Nesting has been observed only a comparatively few times in our history, though the birds may be seen on estuaries and sometimes freshwater lakes when not nesting.

Along the edges of the lakes run black-fronted dotterels and hooded dotterels. Mountain ducks are also salt-lake ducks. Near the sea silver gulls join in the feast of brine shrimps, as do other wading birds.

Although the beds of salt lakes normally remain bare, along the edges grow salt-loving plants; these may range into saltbush steppe, where saltbush (Atriplex) and bluebush (Kochia) dominate. The bluebushes are common round salt pans; about fifty species are found. The name comes from the bluish colour of the succulent leaves. The flowers are not obvious but, when fruiting, the perianths can become quite spectacular in shades of yellow, red or crimson. Saltbushes have grey-green leaves, and both these and the bluebushes are highly regarded by pastoralists as stock food. However, overgrazing has destroyed huge areas of country once covered.

A more spectacular plant is the noonflower, which often forms huge swards of mauve flowers, from coastal salt marshes through to inland deserts. This is a more delicate-looking version of the pigface. The noonflower leaves are cylindrical and succulent, with bright magenta flowers more thickly developed.

Samphires, almost growing in the water, and a feature of salt marshes the world over, belong to the goosefoot family, which also includes the bluebushes.

Salt and bluebush flats cover millions of acres, as on the Nullarbor region, and are therefore an important habitat where trees are almost entirely absent. The most beautiful of the salt marshes are some round Lake Austin in Western Australia. Here, besides the samphires, which often have pinks and other colouring in the leaves, purple peas of Swainsona in good seasons make patches of colour that can be seen from a distance of many miles. These often grow as vines, and one single creeper was found to carry 5,000 flowers. Where winds have blown up dunes of kopai and salt, a few trees may establish. One of these, a strange member of the hibiscus family, seems from a distance to be a cactus. The mature plant, though only three or four feet high, has what appears to be leafless stems. These stems are actually covered by numerous tiny leaves. Hundreds of yellow flowers cover the stems in spring.

This combination of plants creates a fascinating landscape.

10
the growing cathedral
WET SCLEROPHYLL FOREST

This forest many Australians know well, for it is strongly developed in most States. Tall tree trunks are topped with flat leafy crowns to form a canopy. Australia's tallest trees are found here. Sheltered by the green roof, grow smaller trees that need shade. On the forest floor shrubs are common, hardleaved and softleaved. Most characteristic of eastern forest (and missing from the southwest) are the tree ferns. On higher ground, grasses may become more prevalent.

In these wet forests the tallest trees are often a single species. King of all is the mountain ash. This is the world's tallest living hardwood tree. The height record is held by a 322-foot high giant growing in the Styx Valley near Maydena in Tasmania. Three-hundred-foot-high ash are also found in Victoria, and it was here the famous Thorpdale Tree, of 375 feet, was measured in 1880, just before it was cut down. Tasmania and Victoria are the homes of the mountain ash. A similar tree, the alpine ash, is also found in New South Wales. Blackbutt is the dominant tree along the coastlines of New South Wales into southern Queensland. The Sydney bluegum sometimes grows in mixed stands over a slightly lesser range. Northern New South Wales and southern Queensland have the rose gum, and southwestern Australia, the karri.

The eucalypts are the dominating trees of the wet sclerophyll forest, and this applies to the dry sclerophyll. Ninety-five per cent of our commercial forests grow in these two environments; and the wet sclerophyll provides the greatest amount of timber to the acre of any native forest.

In the wet sclerophylls of the eastern States grow tree ferns. Palms are also strongly developed in warmer areas. Tree ferns are quite remarkable. Their rhizomes develop as stout trunks, thickened by aerial roots which also make a good base for epiphytes, including other ferns. The soft tree fern, a Dicksonia, so named because of its brownish soft "hair" growing in the frond butts, is common in the moist gullies. The rough tree fern, which retains rasping frond butts as the dead fronds fall, is found in slightly drier situations often higher on the hill slopes. Tree ferns are also found in rainforest country, and in some forests of dry sclerophyll.

The sclerophyll forests are strong in their growth on both coast and highlands, and shade into rainforest where rainfall becomes heavier and soils suitable.

Brush box are a feature of the transition zones between rainforest and wet sclerophyll. Where the annual rainfall drops below the 45-inch mark, the dry sclerophyll forest begins, though such divisions are not clearcut, for other factors such as soil and aspect become important, as has already been mentioned for other plant communities.

Moving from rainforest to wet sclerophyll to dry sclerophyll one sees an obvious difference—the amount of leaf and other litter on the forest floor. In the rainforest there is a rapid turnover of plant material by the myriads of microscopic animals in the soil, as well as larger animals and plants that use up debris rapidly. Though in the wet forest there is a fairly rapid turnover, in the dry forest, leaf twig and bark litter may accumulate to several feet in thickness.

38

Estimates put the leaf fall from half to one ton an acre each year. This may accumulate until there may be ten tons to the acre on the forest floor—often the reason for disastrous wildfires. If the litter is only about two to three tons to the acre the fire intensity is low.

Animals feed in the litter and graze on the understorey shrubs and on the leaf canopies of the tall trees. Boring insects feed on bark or wood. A single tree may be the entire "earth" for some species. Caterpillars of various leaf miners actually eat the tissues of the leaf, protected by the leaf "skin". Often the foliage is so heavily attacked that it appears scorched. Other species eat the whole leaf, and it is often difficult to find an undamaged leaf on a forest tree. Some grubs attack stems, branches and trunks, either eating the surface or boring in. Gall-making insects produce swellings, where the grubs lie safe surrounded by a veritable mountain of feed. On these insects prey the hunters. These may range from scorpions and shield bearers to frogs, lizards, birds and mammals.

The main animals of the litter, in numbers, are creatures such as mites and springtails, and larger animals such as insect larvae, millipedes, centipedes and spiders. From a naturalist's point of view one of the most interesting of the animals found on the damp floors of forests is the peripatus. This looks something like a velvety caterpillar. Specimens taken in the Blue Mountains near Sydney had 15 pairs of legs. Peripatus attack small creatures in the leaf litter, and if attacked themselves can exude a sticky liquid. Both outside and internal features show that they have some of the characteristics of worms and some of insects, and can be regarded as a link between these major groups.

A less innocent animal is the funnel-web spider. The various species belong to a genus known as *Atrax*, and these occur from Tasmania north into Queensland. All are found in cool, moist places. The horizontal silk-lined tubes or funnels often run under rocks or rotting logs. The female remains in this lair all her life, darting out only to catch food. In captivity she can be fed on raw meat or worms. The male leaves its tunnel when seeking a mate. Funnel-webs have caused at least five human deaths in the Sydney area.

Best known and most popular insects of all forests are the cicadas. The shrill call of the males is a song of summer. Rainforest has a species with a huge abdomen known as the bladder cicada. Naturalist David Fleay described its song as like the sound "of a myriad of tiny bells". In eastern forests are other variations with names such as greengrocer, double drummer, floury miller and black prince.

The life history for most species runs something like this: At the end of the summer season the female cicada lays her eggs on twigs of plants. The eggs hatch in a few weeks, and the babies tumble to the ground and burrow into the soil, where they feed by sucking sap from the roots of host plants. How long they stay underground is a mystery. E. Musgrave, working from cycles of abundance, found that one species has a three-year cycle. An American species is said to live seventeen years underground.

When fully fed, the nymphs tunnel to the surface and wait for the right conditions of humidity and temperature before coming out. Darkness gives them the cover they need for this dramatic change from earth-coloured tunneller to beautiful insect. From the tunnel the insect climbs up the nearest tree, sometimes going only a few feet, sometimes reaching branches twenty feet above ground.

The six legs grip tightly, and under the pressure of the new body the thorax of the old bulges, then splits. The adult emerges with only the tip of the abdomen in contact with its old home. The wing pads are still crumpled but gradually spread and harden. Then the beautiful insect steps away from its old brown pupal case and is ready for its new life.

Cicadas suck the sap of trees, and one tree may be nursery, adult home, and finally grave. Perhaps the males shrill their call to attract females for mating. One species in the Snowy Mountains area is unique in that though it calls, the note is inaudible to human ears; it is also unique in that both male and female make the calls, whereas in other species the female has no song.

In recent years a great deal of study has been made on stick insects. One species has done much damage to the alpine ash as well as to other forest trees. Sometimes the insect eats so much of the canopy that the trees appear to be dying, and so it has earned the name of "ring-barker".

In the outbreaks in the highlands of southeastern Australia there appears to be a two-year cycle for these insects. In the lean years, egg parasites, or birds, or both, keep the insects in check. Birds especially responsible are pied currawongs, blackbacked magpies, ravens, red wattlebirds, noisy friar-birds and blackfaced cuckoo-shrikes. These roam through the forest taking their toll. However, in good years for the insects, the birds still keep on eating as heartily as ever, but there is just too much food. There may be other factors in this, such as the spread of undergrowth fires, for the stick insect eggs are dropped to the forest floor, where they hatch.

Forests at night reveal a world of animal life that lies hidden by day under logs, stones, bark of trees, or other hiding or sheltering places. The geckoes are friendly little lizards. In tropical Australia some live in houses to hunt insects at night across the ceilings. The short, sharp call is startling at first but soon becomes accepted as part of the tropic charm. Geckoes are soft-bodied and, like snakes, lack eyelids. The tongue is used as a kind of windscreen wiper to keep the eyes clean.

Some geckoes have clawed feet, some have broad pads that allow them to appear to defy gravity as they cling to ceilings. These pads are not adhesive in the sucker sense, but covered with hundreds of fine bristles that allow the reptile to cling to tiny irregularities of even "smooth" surfaces.

By day another lizard becomes more obvious in forest country. In the early morning long-tailed, spiky-looking bearded dragons may be seen warming up in a patch of sunlight. It is then they are fairly easily caught. Once thoroughly "hotted" up, they can begin hunting. In trees they find insects that supply much of their food.

If cornered the dragon tries bluff. The huge mouth opens to show the yellow inner lining , a frill of spikes is raised, and the body is flattened to make the reptile appear larger. The bite, though painful, is not dangerous, since the teeth are small and peglike and there is no venom.

A number of snakes are found in forest country. The common or green tree-snake is a harmless species found from New South Wales through Queensland and across northern Australia into the Kimberleys. This snake feeds by day on frogs and other small animals, and will often be found swimming across rivers and creeks in search of food. A backfanged snake, the brown tree snake, though poisonous, is not dangerous to man. It hunts by night, and because of its large eyes is sometimes called the "doll's eye". Both of these snakes when caught give off a strong odour—which no doubt helps in defence.

This wet cool moist forest is perhaps best known for its bellbirds. By "channels of coolness" was how Henry Kendall expressed it, and this is true enough, for the tinkling chimes come from colonies of bellbirds in ferny gullies.

The bellbird, or more exactly bellminer, is a yellow-green honeyeater found from southern Queensland south to Victoria. Slightly smaller than the noisy miner, it has the yellow beak and legs of all the group, and the birds live in colonies. This makes the single "tink" call of each bird into a silvery chime of bells. Seen through binoculars, the bird is a deep olive-green with a small red patch behind the eye.

Another bird of the cool fern gullies, the lyrebird, is found from southern Queensland through to Victoria, and has been introduced to Tasmania. It is interesting that the western-most occurrence in Victoria is in the Kinglake district. Here lies the gap between where the Dividing Range continues into the eastern highlands to the Victorian Alps, and a tangle of forest clad ridges. Westwards the Western Highlands are lower and begin to lack cool fern gullies.

In the rich humus of the forest floor the food of the lyrebird abounds. It consists mainly of worms, insect grubs, centipedes and scorpions. Amphipods, crustaceans known as "hoppers", are also found in the leaf litter.

40

Cheerful inhabitants of the forest country are the pied currawongs, whose bell-like calls ring through the tree-tops. The pied species is found along all the eastern coastal forests—and other species in other parts of forest Australia.

At night, owls hunt through the forest glades—sooty owls, masked owls and, best known of all, the boobook owl. Some owls, like the sooty, are confined to the densely timbered gullies, but the boobook is found throughout most of Australia, even in the arid central country.

A gaily-plumed bird, the crimson rosella, is found in the wet forests mainly of the south-eastern Australian mainland and Tasmania. In these dense forests the birds feed on many kinds of fruits and seeds, especially those of wattles. Should any orchards or farms be near by, rosellas can become a pest. Tourist resorts such as Barrington and Lamington exploit the tameness of these birds, which accept food from the tourists' hands. These birds, from north to south, show interesting variations both in size and colour. A natural history theory, Bergman's Rule, states that warmblooded animals are largest in the cooler parts of their range. Gloger's Rule is that feather pigments are darker in the wetter parts of the range. So desert birds tend to be much lighter in colour, and this becomes obvious to any visitor to inland Australia. Far to the northeast, on the Atherton Tableland, there is a small *dark* population of crimson rosellas.

A harsh screeching in the tree-tops is often the only indication of gaily coloured lorikeets, since these brilliant honeyeating parrots tend to blend with the canopy. The rainbow lorikeet is found across northern Australia, south along the east coast into Tasmania and South Australian forests. Flowering blossoms are the attraction, so these honeyeating birds are nomadic, wandering in search of flowering trees.

Another striking wet-forest bird is the satin bowerbird. The display ground built by the males and decorated with blue and light yellow objects is well known. Recent research by R. A. Vellenga, of Leura, has proved that the male bird is promiscuous, with the bower as his mating ground. Young males watch the older birds and are stimulated to build play bowers. Often a number of immature birds work and display in these. A morning spent in spring watching a bird at its bower can provide one of the most interesting and beautiful sights the bushland has to offer.

At this point it is worth considering the ecology of fire and how it has shaped the plant communties we have been discussing. Certain habitats such as marshes and swamps seem safe from fire, yet even on normally wet lands a prolonged drought may allow fire to penetrate. Rainforest seems safe enough, yet regular firing along the edges not only destroys the outer layers of the forest by heat but allows drying winds to continue the work of destruction.

In Queensland, near Cairns it is easy to see that the rainforest is retreating under the impact of fires from the annual burning in the sugar plantations. At Mount Glorious near Brisbane the reverse holds true. Here strict control of fires is allowing the rainforest to engulf the near-by wet sclerophyll in a green wave. Sydney bluegums and brush box still push their way through the canopy, but when they die there will be no seedlings to take their place. The dark shade of the forest floor means the death of the seeds.

We are only beginning to understand the complexities of the effect of fire on plants and how the patterns of every plant community affect the animal life each contains. Many botanists believe that much of the Australian flora has evolved in adaptation to fire. As we have seen with the heaths, and will see with the mallees, woody underground parts mean that fire prunes the above-ground plant but does not kill it. Eucalypts have dormant buds buried in trunks and larger branches. Many seeds are fire resistant. Some are encased in woody fruits—such as the forest pear or native peach. For many plants a fire is needed to release the seed into a soil enriched by the ash. The ironbarks and other trees have thick barks possibly developed as fire protection. In the karri forest a sunlit ash bed provides good growth of seedlings. Figures for the survival of seedlings are 4,200 to the acre on an ash bed, 1,880 on a clean fair seed bed, and 740 on a poor unfired bed.

The effect of fire on the animals is even less understood, though we know a little more than

41

we did some years ago. In the dry sclerophyll forest it has been found that a native snail occurs in both a light and dark form. Where fires are common, the dark form predominates. It is harder to see in the blackened plant remains, and also burrows deeper. Where fire is kept out, the light form increases.

Similarly, it has been suggested that the Leadbeater's or fairy possum has increased recently. It needs the kind of plant succession provided by a mountain ash forest as it recovers from severe fire. In the heathland country the ground parrot cannot survive if the heath is not fired, for the heath then grows tall and dense; the ideal habitat seems to occur three years after a fire and continues for another three or four years, then the habitat gradually becomes inhospitable once more.

What is good for ground parrots may be disaster for other species. Whether the burn is in spring, summer, autumn or winter will decide what plants dominate—apart from the frequency of the fires.

In one study it was found that the tammar wallaby eats the young seedlings of the rock sheoak. At 5–7 years of age the sheoak becomes shelter for the wallaby; between 11–15 years the tree sheltered phascogales; and, when mature, the ringtail possum. At this stage the woodland becomes dominated by mature sheoaks—and such a habitat provides for the needs of a limited number of animals.

If we wish to keep the variety and excitment of our bushland we need plant mosaics (burning patterns) in most environments.

A Victorian forest officer, A. Hodgson, explains that lack of fire in a mountain ash forest would bring death to the ash from natural causes in from 250 to 350 years. Younger ash trees would not develop, so the forest would be taken over by sassafras and myrtle beech. An occasional fire, while killing the mature ash, allows ash seedlings to develop, so the succession starts once more. A second fire before the seedlings have grown old enough to produce seeds means that bracken and scrub take over.

In a different kind of gum-tree forest, such as in the messmate country, the trees are fire-resistant. A fire brings a healthy crop of legumes and dense thickets. About twenty years later these thickets will have died out, and the floor becomes mainly grass. So the understorey of shrubs needs fires from time to time to keep it in existence.

There are other subtleties in these successions, and it is fascinating for those who live near bushland to watch the changes after fires.

Returning to the story of the animals, one of the possums of the heavily timbered mountains from south Queensland through to Victoria, the bobuck or mountain possum, can be recognized as distinct from smaller brushtail by the small ears. At night it feeds largely on the ground, sampling fallen fruit, shoots, leaves, and then retires to its home among the tall mountain ash, sassafras, beech and hazel.

The fairy possum also lives in these wet forests. Once thought to be extinct, it was rediscovered by naturalist Eric Wilkinson near Marysville in Victoria. The fairy possum is a hunter of insects and possibly a feeder on nectar, and is active and agile. Its home is in the mountain ash and alpine ash country, though it seems to find its most suitable habitat in the thickets of young eucalyptus, wattles and small trees brought on by a fire.

A common animal of the tree-tops from Victoria northwards to mid-Queensland is the greater or dusky glider. Like the koala it is a leaf eater, feeding mainly on gum-leaves.

Fruit bats, also, feed in the tree-tops of the forests, but on nectar rather than leaves. When fruit is ripe or over-ripe the bats will also take to this. Should nectar and native fruits be in short supply, then raids are made on orchards. Native figs in the heart of Sydney are visited at night by bats that roost in a camp along the Lane Cove River.

On the ground, a well-known marsupial, the swamp wallaby, is common in moist gullies from Queensland southwards into South Australia. It also occurs on hillslopes, and even in open forest country, if there is a scrub cover. The brigalow in Queensland is a stronghold.

With this variety of herbivores both on the ground and in the treetops there are also many hunters.

Owls take toll by night and eagles by day. On the ground it was once the Tasman wolf and the Tasmanian devil, with the various native cats that fed well on such animals. Today their place has been taken by the dingo and fox. However, in Tasmania, neither dingo nor fox is to be found, and the devil still prospers. It is a scavenger as well as a killer of live food, and its powerful jaws devour almost every scrap of its victims except the hardest bones. Hunting by night, by day it may be seen sunning itself near its lair. Although most animals are black with a white band on the chest and a white rump patch, black ones are not uncommon, and older animals may be brown.

So the wet schlerophyll forest holds as much interest as the rainforest. Fortunately good samples of it are safe for all time in national parks and nature reserves.

11
the canopied jungle
RAINFOREST

Here we have the most complex nature community the earth has to offer. Dr Len Webb, an Australian authority on rainforest, enthuses that one acre of such forest may contain hundreds of plant species. He tells how, on 18 forest sites in North Queensland, he and his fellow workers collected 818 different plant species. The mind is staggered by the task of finding order in this richness, and has called in the computer to solve problems of classification.

Australians down the years have spoken of this kind of country as jungle, a carry-over from abroad, since rainforest encircles the globe. Another word once used was "brush". This name still lingers in "brush turkey". The most incongruous name is scrub. What a word to describe this magnificent country. Dr Webb was somewhat irritated when I said most Australians had the feeling that rainforest was not really Australian—something alien. He pointed out its *wide* distribution from northern Australia to Tasmania.

The Australian Environment defines rainforest as being a community of trees where the cover forms a continuous canopy. There may be three storeys of trees—at 30, 60, and 100 feet; and at least one of these layers will be continuous. On the ground ferns are common, and epiphytes grow from tree trunks. Climbing lianas grope their way towards the sunlight using the tree trunks as ladders. Most plant leaves are large, and "drip-tips" are common.

There are four main groups of rainforest usually recognized. *Tropical* rainforest has many tree species with buttress roots; lianas are common, and there are many epiphytes. Some taller trees push their way through the continuous top tree layer and may reach heights of 180 feet. With wetter soil, palms dominate the forest. This tropical forest occurs in patches from Cape York south to Gympie, though southwards the tropical forest is seen only at lower levels.

Higher than 2,000 feet, *subtropical* rainforest takes over. This can be found from Cooktown southwards into southern New South Wales and Victoria. Here we have less high tree canopy and more ferns and shrubby plants in the undergrowth.

In patches along northern Australia is a habitat which may be called *monsoon* forest, and here many of the trees are deciduous. In this monsoon country there is a summer wet and a winter dry, so loss of leaves appears as a defence against the winter lack of water rather than cold. Where ground water is permanent, some monsoon forests can become quite exciting places, as at Howard Springs near Darwin.

Temperate rainforest has even fewer tree species, and some tend to dominate. Lianas are not as frequent. In Queensland the temperate rainforest is found only in the high mountains, though southward it can grow at lower levels. In Victoria it is found in sheltered valleys of the Warburtons and the Dandenongs. Sassafras and Antarctic beech are the dominant trees. Tasmania has a strong development of rainforest, and besides these two species, native conifers also grow.

In the *Atlas of Tasmania* W. D. Jackson points out that rainforest and wet sclerophyll have been grouped together because the dividing lines are difficult to show. Fire has been one of the factors that have changed rainforest to other vegetation types. Rainforest covers a large area of Tasmania from sea level to 3,500 feet, and is found as a broad band from north to south with pockets in the northeast and on the east coasts.

Why does rainforest grow only in certain places? As with all plant growth we must consider conditions of soil, aspect, wind, temperature and moisture. Mositure may mean humidity, actual rainfall or the type of drainage.

First and foremost, rainforest is dependent on water, at least fifty inches a year—unless there is a stream or spring. So the forests are found only in areas of high rainfall, yet this is not the whole story. In Queensland, where the winds are southeast trades, or northwest monsoons punctuated by up to half a dozen cyclones, rainforests can be found in all kinds of localities where the rain is sufficient. Southeastern Australia, with dry westerly winds in the winter, has its rainforests restricted to the eastern aspects of ranges, or sheltered gullies.

Cold does not stop rainforest—as we have seen with its growth in Tasmania, though frosts and snow are fatal to it. Soil is a factor, since most rainforests grow in rich loams, though deep sandy soils can also carry forests.

Finally we must consider the evolutionary reason that—in theory at least—some hundred million years ago, when the flowering plants developed, Australia became the home of what we regard as typically our plants—gum trees, banksias, tea trees and wattles, though not all of these are confined to our continent. Trees like Antarctic beech and conifers, which may have covered the wetter eastern areas with temperate rainforest, and which botanists call the Antarctic element, possibly developed when the continental masses were together and sharing plants and animals. When Australia drifted northwards, a third element came in—the tropical rainforest. For this reason such plant groups are confined to northern and eastern Australia, cut off by arid barriers from the rest of the country. Temperate rainforest survived on the moister southeast coast, and so provided a barrier to the tropical plants.

Already something will have been gathered of the look of a rainforest. With a continuous canopy little light reaches the forest floor, perhaps one two-hundredth of that in open country. When a large tree dies, or around the edges of such forests, a tangle of shrubs and seedling trees develops. Finally one triumphs and shuts off the light once more. Many people mistake this tangle of vegetation along the fringes of rainforest as being typical of the forest itself.

This is not so. Rainforest is often as easy to walk through as any open forest. Walking through it quickly reveals such characteristics as lack of wind, high humidity, stable temperatures as well as the subdued light. Trees that succeed to finally form the canopy then have to face strong sunlight, wind and lower humidities. This is why many rainforest trees thrive on their own as street or garden trees.

The feature of a rainforest that strikes any visitor is the general similarity of tree trunks because of the dense growth of lichens, mosses and other plants. Flat buttress roots are also evident. Some botanists think these are stabilizing structures, with the same purpose as the flying buttresses used to strengthen the walls of mediaeval churches. Then there are the long trailing, looping vines. The lawyer vine is well known, since it clings with recurved hooks. Some of these lianas are the longest land plants, a few reaching six or seven hundred feet.

And everywhere are the epiphytes, plants growing on the trunks or branches of trees, yet not parasitic in any sense. Many are ferns, such as the well-known birds'-nest, staghorn, and elkhorn ferns, with orchids in profusion.

The plant leaves themselves are fascinating. Large and green, they are the typical leaves found on moisture-loving plants. Many have "drip tips" which no doubt help to keep excessive moisture off the leaf blade.

All this makes a picture of vigorous growth. Leaves and other ground litter are quickly returned to the soil by the activity of fungi and other life. This is in contrast to the drier forests where leaf litter may become thick, or monsoon forests where in the dry winter a thick carpet of yellow leaves gives the whole land a striking appearance.

Judging by the age of the larger trees it takes about five hundred years for a climax rainforest to establish. This makes nonsense of statements by mining companies that they can "restore" mined forest areas. Obviously the restoration of a rainforest is a long process and impossible if the whole forest is destroyed through mining.

Perhaps the trees that excite most interest are the strangler figs. Here the fruit, falling into a crevice high up in a tree, sends roots towards the ground and a shoot upwards. More and more roots develop until the host is enfolded in a strangling cage of roots. Finally the host tree dies, killed by the fig. The trunk slowly rots, leaving the fig tree. A well-known tourist attraction is the curtain fig in North Queensland, where the original seedling started to grow on a leaning host. Instead of developing a strangling cage, the roots formed a double curtain. Some figs grow in the banyan pattern, where secondary trunks develop surrounding the primary original trunk.

On another note are the stinging trees. We have three species of this *Laportea* genus, and these are found in most of the tropical and subtropical rainforests. The giant stinging tree can grow to a height of 100 feet; the Gympie bush is a tall shrub, said to have more "hairs" than the others. The hairs inject a poison when brushed by bare skin. Fortunately there have been no deaths recorded from stings in Australia, though a serious condition arises if a large area of skin is affected.

Well-known garden trees such as the mock orange, pittosporum, white cedar, silky oak, flame tree and the wheel-of-fire tree are rainforest natives. There are also important timber trees such as maple, red cedar, hoop pine, and coachwood.

Dr L. Webb in *The Last of Lands* discusses Australian plants and chemical research. He stresses the importance of rainforest plants as a source of drugs. For example, a scrub ash of the rainforest contains alkaloids, one of which has given a new lead in cancer research. He mentions another tree whose bark was chewed by New Guinea natives before they went fighting, as well as used in producing "dreams about the future". Eight useful alkaloids have been obtained from it. It is quite possible that dreaded plants like stinging trees, finger cherries, and the like, which are now destroyed, will one day become important. Dr Webb cites a similar tree, the Calabar bean of Nigeria, which today produces an export drug.

Unless we keep sufficient of all kinds of rainforest and other habitats as national parks and nature reserves we might well lose any chance of investigating the medicinal and other values of our plants. It would be a tragedy if short-sighted greed and ignorance overlook the long-term dividends from such places.

Orchids also grow in rainforests. One that grows on the Antarctic beech is known as the beech orchid. Although not entirely confined to beech, this orchid is always found near these trees—the favoured host. It is found only from forests in mid-New South Wales to south-eastern Queensland. The Antarctic beech trees make extraordinarily striking forests. The cool green glades formed by these trees are wildly picturesque, with huge boles some ten feet across. Trees often throw up several trunks. The boles are a riot of green mosses and lichens, with many epiphytes. Dead trunks persist for many years and develop huge bracket fungi sometimes a foot across.

In Tasmania grows another species—more of a shrub, and being deciduous it provides colourful stands in autumn. Myrtle beech is dominant in the Tasmanian rainforests and also occurs in Victorian gullies.

In the past, fires lit by both Aboriginal and white people slowly destroyed the edges of the rainforests. Where fire protection is given the rainforest is now extending over the wet sclerophyll forest. In the dim light of the forest floor eucalyptus seedlings cannot grow. The introduced lantana tends to flourish in the burned zones on the edge of the rainforest.

Tropical rainforests have proved resistant to human occupation. The Australian Aborigines did manage to obtain a certain amount of food from such places. The bunya pine's huge cones were eagerly sought by the local Aborigines in an annual pilgrimage to the bunya areas.

The only food plant Australia has provided for the world—the popple-nut or Macadamia—

grows in rainforest. These plants have been grown successfully in Hawaii, which provides most of the nuts used in the world today.

As for animals, rainforests provide a bewildering variety, but lack the spectacular forms found on other continents. Australian rainforests lack any flesheater larger than a dingo or tiger cat. However, persistent stories about a "marsupial tiger" may mean that a large animal still remains to be identified in such places.

Among the mammals there is a rich assortment of possums, including the extraordinary green ringtail.

Also, in the trees, are found two kinds of kangaroos—in northeastern Queensland. Strong curved claws on the forelegs and roughened soles on the hind, enable the tree kangaroo to climb among trees, though it still retains the kangaroo's bound when on the ground.

There are other tree dwellers; the monkey-like cuscus is the most spectacular. Huge bats, known as flying foxes or fruit bats, are largely nectar feeders, though soft fruit is also relished. The camps of these bats high in rainforest trees are a medley of noise by day. At dusk the now-silent animals fly off to feeding grounds. Since there may be several hundred thousand bats in such a camp, it is an awesome sight when the whole sky seems filled with animals.

On the ground is the remarkable musk kangaroo, a puzzle for scientists. It feeds by day, as does the red-legged pademelon wallaby. Dingoes also move by day in the dim light of the rain-forest floor.

The most obvious inhabitants, the birds, provide most interest. Giant among these is the cassowary, the huge helmeted bird found only in North Queensland. Though not as tall as the emu, it is heavier, and the powerful feet carry sharp claws on the inner toes. At least one human death has occurred in Australia, when an attacked bird retaliated. Deaths also happen occasionally in New Guinea when hunted birds, or those having their young threatened, defend themselves. Fruit fallen from the trees through ripeness, or dislodged by feeding fruit bats or pigeons, provides most of the food for cassowaries. The "crash-helmet" on the head is useful in pushing away undergrowth, and possibly it has a secondary use in display, together with the wattles of blue and scarlet carried on the head. Cassowaries are more often heard than seen, as they grunt and grumble and crash through the undergrowth.

Another bird of the ground, the brush turkey, is found from near Sydney northwards, in forest country. Like the mallee fowl, it is a mound builder, a heap of leaves being scraped together to make a low mound about twelve feet in diameter. The heat of the decaying vegetation keeps the eggs warm in a natural incubator.

Yet even such mounds are dwarfed by the nests of the smaller jungle-fowl, found across northern Australia to central Queensland. Sometimes this bird may lay an egg in a hole in a sand-beach, but usually in a huge mound, perhaps ten feet or more high and forty feet in diameter. Again the mound is made partly of leaves, and so becomes a natural incubator for the eggs.

In the treetops may be seen various birds of paradise. Australia has four species, and one is found as far south as the Hunter River in New South Wales, though Queensland is the stronghold. There are rainforest pigeons and parrots, bright additions to the fauna.

Among reptiles carpet snakes are common as they climb trees in search of prey or glide along the ground to find a new hunting place. The giant of the reptiles is the scrub or amethyst python, so named because of the colour of the scales of the freshly moulted snake. There is much legend about the length of these reptiles, and though not the largest of the world's snakes, they would be fifth or sixth. Eric Worrell recorded that one animal he caught dis-gorged "a bush rat, a long-nosed bandicoot and a whistling kite", showing its range of food. Wallabies are also a favoured food.

In such a moist environment there are many frogs, the introduced cane toad, and masses of insects and other inhabitants of the leaf litter and rich mould. There are millipedes, pill bugs, cockroaches, trapdoor spiders, and land crustaceans called woodhoppers. Even freshwater crayfish may go wandering overland from pools. A less pleasant animal of the moist ground is the leech. A boot-full of blood is often the first introduction to this bloodsucking worm. However, a little blood lost to a leech is a small price to pay for the fascinations of the rain-forest habitat.

ROCK SUCCESSIONS *usually have lichens as a second stage. "Bare" rock, rarely is bare. A micro-scope reveals much life. The first colonizers are bacteria; then algae, which often give rocks a black appearance when dry. Plants sometimes form co-operatives, and the best known is the lichen, where algae and fungi live together in a symbiotic relationship. These orange lichens can be seen growing steadily outwards as they colonize new parts of the rock.*

On top of Ayers Rock, a "bare" rock surface, under attack by water, air and heat. Organisms growing on the surface help to break off particles to form soil. When this is deep enough bigger plants can grow. Here acacias up to ten feet high are seen, surviving at the end of a seven-year drought, apparently from occasional showers stored in the thin layer of soil. Even the hardest of rock surfaces crumbles in time, to finally disappear under a green wave of vegetation.

Pioneer animals like this skink find a home through rock succession. Some rocks by their basic structure become deeply shattered by joints. This speeds up the erosion of the rock, since weathering agents can penetrate more deeply. Animals and plants find niches for living. The rock-haunting Cunningham's skink hides in crevices and ventures to near-by places in search of food such as insects.

SALT LAKES *become the home of mountain ducks at Rottnest in Western Australia. Some animals are found only in one habitat; others range over many, but are often regarded as being typical of a particular habitat. Mountain ducks are looked on as creatures of salt-lakes and estuaries, though they must find freshwater for drinking.*

WET SCLEROPHYLL FOREST, *it has been suggested recently, should be called tall open forest. This is a habitat where tall trees, sometimes over two hundred feet, provide a canopy, though not a completely closed one. Enough light comes through the fairly open roof to the forest floor to allow growth of tall shrubs and trees such as palms and tree-ferns. Closer to the ground are more ferns, and lush plants. Today such forests do not survive for as long as they did in the past, since wildfires often destroy the dominant trees.*

Sugar gliders may be seen in the wet sclerophyll forest. They range also into the more open woodlands, and feed on blossoms and insects and other small animals of the canopy. Sugar gliders also bite into branches and drink the sap from the trees. Hollows in trees serve as nests. Gliders are very vocal.

RAINFOREST *is a closed forest formation. Its dense canopy prevents most light from reaching the forest floor. The coming of the Aborigines with their fires led to shrinkage of rainforest in some parts. White men brought more destruction; but protection is now increasing the extent of forest. At Mount Glorious, Queensland, for instance, a central patch of grey-green eucalypt forest is being slowly engulfed by richer-coloured rainforest. Though individual tall gumtrees survive, no young plants can develop. The darkness and moisture do not allow their successful growth, though these conditions are ideal for rainforest tree seedlings.*

With little direct light on the forest floor, rainforest provides an ideal growing place for fungi. These plants lack all green chlorophyll, and therefore must live by feeding on other living things. The fungus body consists of feeding threads that penetrate the food store, then develop the fruiting bodies, which spread the spores—and from these new fungi grow. The yellow brackets are fruiting bodies. The feeding threads rapidly destroy the fallen tree, unlocking its food store for other plants of the rainforest.

12
the best-known forest
DRY SCLEROPHYLL

With less rainfall and often poorer soil, wet sclerophyll forest changes to dry sclerophyll. The structure is similar to that of the wet forest, with flat-topped crowns forming an almost continuous cover, though since the dominant trees are mainly eucalyptus and angophoras, the nature of the leaves and their habit of hanging vertically allows far more light to reach the forest floor, in contrast to the deep shade of the rainforests.

In the dry forest there are usually smaller trees such as sheoaks and banksias, and on the ground an assortment of hard-leaved plants, many with small spiny leaves.

This is the best-known forest to most Australians.

From the timber point of view the dry sclerophyll forests are dominated by jarrah in south-western Australia, messmate stringybarks and brown stingybarks in South Australia and Victoria, and spotted gums in New South Wales and Queensland.

The ground plants are equally varied. Three typical ones are bracken fern, grass trees and cycads. Bracken fern is common in moister areas—and found all over the world, a tribute to its toughness. Its rhizomes are hardy and run underground, where they are safe from most attacks of animals. The growth in spring and summer stores food in the rhizomes, and from this starts a fresh growth in the spring. These underground parts grow at three levels, and with good conditions a single plant can cover an acre in one year. This manner of spread is probably more important than the normal fern reproduction by spores.

Grass trees, also known as blackboys and yaccas, are striking plants found in every State. Western Australia has most of the 16 Australian species.

Some develop large trunks covered with the bases of the dead leaves. Some throw up only a crown of leaves and in season a flowering spike. The rather slow-growing Kingia has a number of flowering heads like drumsticks, and this plant is reputed to grow only an eighth of an inch a year. Other grass trees grow about an inch a year. Most have a large amount of resin, and this has from time to time been used in industry. Picric acid, lacquers and firework material are some of its products. Flowering is irregular but often stimulated by bushfires, and brings a host of insects. Honeyeating birds and mammals come to feed on the spike—and hunters of these animals come to catch them.

Interesting plants of the forest floor are the various species of cycads. These are a family of plants that look very much like palms but are a much older group believed to be the link between ferns and flowering plants. They are among the most primitive of the seed-bearing plants. Three main groups occur in Australia—Cycas, Macrozamia, and Bowenia.

The cycads have the bad reputation of being poisonous to people and stock. Aborigines when using the seeds for food treated these with water to remove the poison. Cycads are slow-growing, and one in Queensland, named Grandfather Peter, was believed to be between 1,000 and 1,500 years old. Vandals destroyed this plant, but in southwestern Australia is a cycad that may be even older. Working on zamia growing in my garden I studied the rate at which new leaves were produced. Then by counting leaf bases made a rough estimate of the age of the plants. For one very large plant I estimated the age at 14,000 years. Zamia could well be the oldest living thing on earth.

The jarrah forest can be taken as an example of a typical dry forest. Once it covered over thirteen million acres in the southwest. The rainfall in this region is 30 to 50 inches, falling mostly in winter. In the wetter southwest corner jarrah forest merges with wet sclerophyll karri forest, and to the east it merges with woodland. Four million acreas of this forest are now protected for timber value, and another one and a half million acres are still held as vacant Crown Land.

Although jarrah is dominant, marri, blackbutt and flooded gum grow with it. The under-storey is mainly bull banksia and forest sheoak. On the forest floor are harsh-leaved shrubs as well as the blackboys and cycads.

Jarrah is recognized as one of the eucalyptus that resist fire best. Light fires release seeds, and winter rains germinate these. The seedling remains as a small shrub until it has grown an underground woody stock, a lignotuber about 3–4 inches in diameter. This may take ten to twenty years. If another fire opens out the canopy a single shoot begins to grow into the mature tree.

By this time the mature tree has developed a bark up to one and a half inches thick. A fire may scorch this or cause big flakes to fall, or sometimes send burning torches of bark flying into the sky to start spot fires farther on. The tree, by its dormant buds in the bark, can coppice freely after fire. A mature tree after cutting can still send up shoots. So here we have a tough species able to handle the worst conditions of fire.

Leaves and barks fall to the floor at the rate of about one ton to the acre each year. This provides for the development of a varied fauna. One study of jarrah forest litter by P. J. McNamara showed that incredible numbers of small animals occur. In an acre of litter there could be on the average about forty million. Of these, mites and springtails make up about eighty six per cent, millipedes and centipedes one and a half per cent, larvae of insects about four and a half per cent, and other animals about eight per cent.

In terms of weight of the larvae and adult insects, millipedes, centipedes and others make up about ninety per cent of the animal life present. Animals such as earthworms, which occur in hundreds of thousands to the acre in northern forests, are much less plentiful here. So too are woodlice. Among the insect larvae found most are those of flies of one kind or another, and the rest mainly of wasps and beetles. Scarabs, chafers and weevils are the commonest of the beetles. Adult insects, particularly beetles and flies, are also found.

Such small animals help break down the leaf litter—though they cannot keep pace with the normal fall of litter. An encouraging feature is that firebreaks burned each year still have a large amount of life, in this instance, over half the figures for the unburned areas.

An interesting pattern with one inhabitant of the forest floor has been discovered by Professor A. R. Main, working with a native snail found in Kings Park, a nature reserve in the heart of Perth. One particular species occurred in two colour forms—a yellow shelled and a dark shelled. With the controlled regular fires that take place in the park, the ground in the jarrah-banksia zones in this particular forest becomes black and bare, though later leaf fall provides some cover. Birds like magpies can forage through the forest floor, and it appears at this time that yellow snails are seen and eaten though the black forms escape. Over the years this means that the yellow form remains common in the tuart areas where fires tend to only scorch the edges and the snail merges into the ground pattern. So here is an example of how the presence or absence of fire can favour one or other colour forms of this snail. Fascinating patterns are being discovered for animals encouraged by the effects of fire.

Among the wealth of life found in forests, and in particular trees such as the river red gums of the Darling and other places in dry Australia, are the cup moths. The strangely shaped caterpillars have earned various names such as Chinese junks or tanks. The gaily-coloured grub shuffles along very much like an army tank—and even more warlike are tufts of stinging

50

hairs that project from tubercles at each end. The grubs are eaten by birds such as crows, yet despite all attacks, in some years trees may be stripped of most of their leaves by the caterpillars. When mature the larvae spin beautiful cocoons that look like a large round egg. When the moth emerges a circular lid is hinged back, and so the resemblance to a tiny cup is seen.

One of the most noticeable traces of insects in eastern forests, which range from wet to woodland, is on the scribble gums. Many species are attacked by the larvae of various insects, mainly moths and beetles. The larvae tunnel under the bark, leaving behind a scribble showing where they have fed. In smoothbarked gums these marks make attractive patterns after bark is shed, but in stringybarks the scribbles can be seen only when the tree is cut and the bark removed.

Nearer the forest floor are hunters of small creatures, and most noticeable in many types of forest are the various species of golden orb-weavers. These plump-bodied spiders build webs of golden silk, strong enough to hold small birds. Still closer to the forest floor and common in both wet and dry gum forests are the rolled leaf spiders. Here the adult spider makes a home in the centre of its web by rolling a leaf into a tube. Sometimes it may use a piece of paper or even an empty snail shell as a home.

On the forest floor and climbing the trunks of trees are the millipedes, many legged creatures that feed on leaf litter. The cylindrical bodies have numerous legs sometimes running into hundreds; and though lacking poison jaws the millipedes gain protection through an unpleasant taste.

Well able to protect themselves on the forest floor are the bullants. These inch-long insects have a sting that can kill enemies three times their size and make even people keep a respectful distance. Nests are usually placed near trees, and the ants climb these to gather nectar—their main food. For the bullant larvae the workers capture honeybees, but will also take grasshoppers and other insects.

Under the bark of trees the marbled geckoes hide by day to emerge and hunt for insects by night. Sometimes in the forest litter or under the bark may be found two small white eggs of this lizard.

Another lizard dwelling under the bark of trees or under stones is the barking gecko, an attractively marked lizard and a doughty fighter. When alarmed it stands stiffly on long, thin legs and barks at its enemy. It will also leap forward and bite hard on an intruding finger, but human skin is too tough to be broken by this bite.

The large tree goanna or lace monitor ranges through the trees. This common lizard of eastern Australia occurs in two main varieties. Some are black with bands of yellow spots, and on others the bands become continuous. Goannas are useful animals in the bush, devouring small snakes, rabbits, fox cubs and carrion of all kinds as well as any other small creatures they can catch. Like all Australian lizards, they do not have a poisonous bite.

Another dweller in trees is the carpet snake. All pythons are good climbers, and the carpet snake may often be seen resting on the branches of a forest tree.

The carpet snake ranges widely. In coastal New South Wales it is greenish black, patterned in yellow spots, and is known as the diamond snake—actually a close relative of the carpet snake, whose patterning is much more striking, with patches of dark brown edged with black. Both eat small mammals and birds they catch in the trees and on the ground.

A lizard common in the dry forest (and found in other places) is the bluetongue. Closely related species occur in most parts of Australia. The half dozen bluetongue species belong to a family of lizards known as skinks. Skinks all have fairly smooth bodies and are the largest of the world's lizard families—not in size, because that honour goes to the goanna family, but in number of species. Australia has about a hundred kinds of skinks, and they range from the small shiny lizards that sun themselves on rocks and fence-posts to the giant bluetongues and others that may reach two feet in length. Most skinks have an interesting habit of breaking off the tail when frightened. An enemy making a grab at the reptile often finds it has a wriggling tail but no head or body. The lizard has a device by which it can fracture away the tail and at the same time seal off the blood vessels. While the pursuer is busily devouring the tail, the lizard makes good its escape. Later it can grow a new one, not as decorative as the old but serviceable enough.

A common inhabitant of the forest floor—though its work is more often seen than the animal itself—is the echidna. This egg-laying mammal is built like a small bulldozer—very strong and able to shift heavy weights. Although armed with sharp spikes and ability to coil into a ball, most echidnas when alarmed prefer to burrow into the soil, particularly among tree roots. Once wedged they are almost impossible to move. Their strong digging claws are used for tearing open termite mounds to find insects on which the echidna feeds. Ant mounds too are broken open, the meat ants being particularly favoured in the springtime when the nests are full of winged ones.

In captivity echidnas have lived for fifty years, so possibly longevity as well as the armour of spikes has made the echidna a much more successful animal than many other natives.

A great deal has been discovered about this animal in the last few years. Some time ago Queensland naturalist David Fleay reported the observations of Ann Miller, of Tara. This fortunate woman had been able to watch something that had baffled scientists for years. She observed how the mother echidna developed her pouch, and how long it took for the baby to hatch. The echidna, like the platypus, is an egglaying mammal, but the spiky echidna, unlike the platypus, does not build a nest in a burrow. She develops a fold of skin on the abdomen. Anne Miller picked up the mother in late August. Over the next nine days a pouch developed, and by early September an egg had been laid. Echidna eggs are very small, only about half an inch across, and are laid directly into the pouch, for the echidna has a very flexible body.

Nine days after the egg-laying Anne Miller took another look, and by this time the pouch was beautifully developed. Two days later the baby had hatched, though unfortunately it died after about a week. David Fleay himself managed to raise such a baby for six weeks, until an intruding cat caused its death. One authoritative book on mammals says the baby is kept in the pouch for about eight weeks, then the mother puts her child into a sheltered spot, and returns to feed it.

The grey kangaroo, the largest of marsupials, belongs to the forest country along both the eastern and southern areas. Two species of grey occur here. In Tasmania it is known as the forester, but animals can be found well into the woodlands. On the plains it is replaced by the red.

Among the possums, the brushtail replaces the mountain possum of the wet forests. (In Tasmania the mountain possum does not occur; a race of the brushtail has moved in to this niche.) Brushtails feed mainly on the trees, mostly on mature leaves. When fire cuts down the amount of food, they may feed on ground plants. Even after the devastating bushfires in Tasmania some years ago, in tiny patches of unburned bush possums managed to survive. Unlike the mountain possum, which not only feeds but also lives in ground retreats, the brushtail commonly lives in holes in dead or growing trees. Ringtail possums, with a slender tail and white tip, include various species. Ringtails are found in all types of forest country through to open woodland.

Gliders, marsupials that are able to glide from tree to tree by means of skin membranes stretching along the sides of the body, appear in the forests. Sugar gliders are the most widespread, and found throughout the forest and woodland country of northern and eastern Australia. They were introduced to Tasmania. Besides feeding on insects, the sugar gliders also eat nectar. An unusual food supply is obtained by chewing into the bark of the trees to tap the sap flow, a habit shared by other gliders.

Of the complete flesh-eaters, the mainland forests have no large marsupial to be compared with the Tasmanian tiger. This animal was once common on the mainland, judging by fossils in caves. Possibly the coming of the dingo meant the last of the tiger. The marsupial tiger cat is found along the eastern forests into Tasmania and has a two-foot-long body with a tail about the same length. A male may weigh up to seven pounds. The related native cats are much smaller, and various species are found over much of Australia, though the southeastern species is now found only in any numbers in Tasmania, and may be close to extinction on the mainland.

A simple distinguishing feature is that though both tiger and native cats are spotted, on the tiger the spots continue to the tail where the hairs are short. Native cats have shorter unspotted tails, and the longer hairs tend to give a brush-like appearance.

Much more obvious in the forest than the mammals are the birds. And most obvious of birds are members of the parrot group. Nectar feeding lorikeets race in screeching flocks across the sky, and longtailed parrots and broadtailed cockatoos add to the clamour. Birds well known both in the wilds and as pets are the sulphur-crested cockatoos. These noble white birds are found in forests throughout northern and eastern Australia, as well as Tasmania. Even coastal mangroves may shelter them, and they are also to be found in rainforests, wet and dry sclerophyll, and woodlands, as well as riverside trees. As seed-eaters they cause trouble to farmers, both by digging sown seed and attacking ripe crops. But their diet includes a wide variety of native seeds, berries and fruits as well as other plant parts such as corms.

Equally widespread are the ringneck parrots, which can be found from the dense coastal forest through the woodlands to mulga and desert country. They are greenish, with a narrow ring of yellow round the neck. Some authorities separate them into a number of species, one kind called the twentyeight, from its ringing call. It is found in southwestern Australia, at Port Lincoln in South Australia, and in central Australia. Farther to the eastern inland is the mallee ringneck.

Bird predators are common, including a number of hawks and eagles. On a small scale is the grey butcherbird. Butcherbirds, magpies and currawongs are usually considered members of one family of birds, and found mainly in Australia. All eat a variety of food and supplement their diet with other small creatures such as mammals and birds. The butcherbird gets its name from its habit of creating a larder by impaling prey on tree spikes or forks. Sometimes as many as six silvereyes may be hung up in this way. All members of the family are noted for their sonorous calls, the western magpies possibly the finest songsters of all.

A hunter by night in forest country, the boobook owl shelters by day in a cluster of leaves on a tree branch. Its double-noted call was often mistaken by the early colonists for that of a cuckoo; they discovered later that the boobook note came from a hawk-owl.

These dry forests of Australia provide a wealth of interest to naturalists. Since most of the densely populated areas of Australia were set up in such habitats, the dry forest country and the woodlands, are the best known of all.

13
natural parks
WOODLAND

Here we have trees with the "woodland" form—in the shape we know from city parks, with the boles not quite as long as the crown depth. The trees are wider spread, and may vary from almost touching to wide-spaced. The shape is that drawn by children when asked to draw a tree, and this is the shape most take when isolated either by nature or artificial clearing. Even a tall karri from the wet sclerophyll grows in the woodland form if planted in a garden.

The ground cover varies, and woodland is divided into a number of subforms. Here we can look on the areas between the forest country and the dry interior as a woodland community. It does not continue unbroken round Australia; there are gaps filled with mulga scrub, mallee, grassland and saltbush.

The woodland floor may be mainly grasses, in the savannah woodlands, or elsewhere hard shrubs. There are great variations over Australia in the kinds of trees to be found. Woodlands of northern Australia are dominated by bloodwoods—such as stringybarks and woolly butts. Grasses develop strongly, and a feature of the northern lands are the regular fires that sweep this country and turn it from a grey green woodland with yellow grasses, to a forest with a black floor. In more temperate regions the boxes, apple boxes, and red gums become important. In the high country snow gums are the main tree. South-western Australia has on the limestone country near the coast a valuable timber tree, tuart, with an understorey of peppermint. Inland grows the wandoo.

In drier areas, particularly in New South Wales and Queensland, grow strong developments of white cypress pine on sandy soils. Cypress stands also occur in the Northern Territory

In general the woodlands are a pleasing forest that allow easy walking. Although the wild-life may not be so great as in better-watered lands, the open nature of the country makes observation easier. Marsupials, birds, reptiles and insects can readily be seen. The same applies even more in the dry centre country, as the decrease in height of the trees and the lessening of the ground cover let most animals be viewed with ease. A kangaroo bounding over open country may be seen many miles off, but in the dry sclerophyll forest it melts into invisibility at a distance of twenty yards.

It would be impossible here to deal with more than a few of the plants of the woodlands. The woolly-butt of northern Australia, which with the Darwin stringbark is the common eucalypt of the northern forests, is so named because of the spongy grey bark at the base of the tree. High on the bole this flakes off to give a smooth white bark. Woolly-butts grow to about eighty feet in height. This makes them one of the few trees suitable for mill timber. In the flowering season, scarlet or orange blossoms attract masses of honeyeaters and lorikeets.

In the south-west corner of the continent, wandoo grows on the clay soils of woodlands. A relative, the powderbark wandoo, grows in the poorer laterite soils, and the two provide an attractive picture, with bark of various shades from white, through to orange and red. The powderbark is the more brilliant in colouring; but both give a fascinating character to the woodland. Economically the wandoo is important for both its timber and its tannin. Not only the bark supplies tannin; the wood yields eight per cent of this, and the whole tree apart from the leaves can be used. With a local charcoal iron plant, there can be a complete use of the tree. Also there is a good nectar flow—with yields of up to 200 pounds of honey from a hive not uncommon in good years. The sub-alpine woodlands of snow gum will be discussed in the alpine section.

Yellow box is another woodland tree well distributed, from Victoria through New South Wales on the western side of the divide, and into south-eastern Queensland. Good for timber, and also as a honey tree, it has some of the virtues of the wandoo.

Some interesting patterns of the woodlands can be seen in the life of the *birds* in the marri; that of the *wasps* and grubs in eastern woodlands; and that of the *complex wildlife* at a small reserve called Tutanning.

The marri, an important tree in the dry sclerophyll forests of the southwest, is also found in the woodlands. When land clearing takes place, marris are often left for their shade and appearance. Grasses will grow right to the base of the trunk. Naturalist Angus Robinson has made a study of these trees on his own property, and also in untouched woodlands. The tree usually flowers in late summer, and the amount of blossom varies from year to year. Legend has it that a heavy flowering means a wet winter to come, but there is no evidence of this. He found that cool conditions stimulated a good honey flow, and dry winds cut it short.

An extraordinary number and diversity of animals come for the flow of nectar. Among the birds are black cockatoos, redcapped parrots, twentyeight parrots, and purple-crowned lorikeets. Many of these birds are nomads following the flowering. Honeyeaters such as red wattlebirds, singing honeyeaters and others are common, and silvereyes also share in the feast.

Feeding on insects attracted to the blossoms are blue wrens, various thornbills, western warblers, rufous whistlers, grey fantails, magpies, butcher birds and crows.

Birds feeding on the fruit offer a good example of avian evolution. The fruit develops as a soft green structure gradually growing to over an inch in length and diameter until finally it matures into a hardy woody fruit. All stages can be found on the same tree. Twentyeight parrots chop into this fruit, from the side, while it is still green, and eat both cone and seeds. The redcapped parrot more efficiently cuts through to the seed chamber from the top, and devours the seeds. With the hardening of the fruit new techniques are needed. Now the seed can only be obtained through the lip of the fruit. Twentyeights disappear, but the redcapped parrot comes in. This bird, with its very long upper bill, is able to hold the fruit and pick out the seeds. Marks are left by the lower bill as the bird grips the fruit while taking out the seeds. The more powerful bill of the black cockatoo is also able to rifle the seed store, though in a cruder way, by breaking it open from the sides.

In eastern woodlands it has been found that control of some grubs that attack pastures is linked with the trees. Parasitic wasps normally control such pests by laying eggs in the caterpillars. The young on emerging eat their host. The adult wasps however also need food. This is provided by nectar in the tree blossoms. If the trees go, then the wasps go. Even so, a little grass root pruning by insect grubs can stimulate growth. It is only when the pruning becomes too heavy, because of too many underground grubs, that pastures suffer. Thus we see how completely clearing savannah woodlands may be an inefficient way of improving pastures.

Tutanning Reserve, though only about four thousand acres, is a mixture of habitats, and has been closely studied by scientists under the leadership of Professor A. R. Main. On offshore islands of comparable size only one species of wallaby occurs, yet this small area holds grey kangaroos, brush wallabies, tammars, bettongs, bandicoots, brushtail and ringtail possums, numbats and phascogales.

Many such reserves are "islands" in a sea of farmland or other development, and are recently created. In time the diversity of species they hold will become less, until they have only a fraction of their present richness. So the aim of research is to find how to keep the diversity. The main problems are food, shelter and water.

Shelter and food are not necessarily provided by the same plant. For instance, dryandras in the area are prickly and not favoured as food by the marsupials; but they make thickets to shelter tammar wallabies and some bettongs. The food for these animals are grasses, annuals, and shrubs. These may be some distance away from the lateritic ridges where the dryandras grow. Also the kind of firing pattern decides what kind and height of plants grow, so both soils and fire affect the reserve. To add more complexity, there is a rock sheoak which as a seedling is food for the tammar wallaby. At five to seven years of age it forms a thicket that shelters the wallaby, and at between eleven and fifteen years it becomes the habitat of the phascogales. When it is a mature tree, the ringtail possum moves in. After 30 years the woodland is almost entirely sheoak; the shorter-lived shrubs have died out.

Work in other areas shows that tammar wallabies can survive on a territory of four and a half acres: but the much smaller bettong needs 50 acres at Tutanning. This shows how much research work is essential in all kinds of habitats to find what the needs of our animals are.

A showy insect known as the emperor gum moth is seen in eastern and western woodlands. The common eastern kind has a large bluish-green caterpillar, and the cocoon may shelter the pupa for several years before the handsome moth, with its large eye-spots, emerges.

Woodlands offer a wealth of life among smaller creatures, insects and spiders, including a fascinating variety of trapdoor spiders; yet the most obvious creature is the processionary caterpillar. The long furry lines of grubs in autumn arouse curious comment, and the huge silken bags festooning gums and wattles are seen all the year round. The adult female moths lay bundles of eggs on the branchlets of food trees. The grubs hatch, feed on the leaves by night, and by day retreat to the safety of a bag that has been spun communally. As the grubs grow larger, the bag is enlarged till by the end of a season it may be the size of a small football, packed with the droppings of the grubs as well as cast-off skins. It is these that give the bag its major protection since the hairs of the skins are irritating in the extreme. Cattle have died through licking-up these hairs when feeding on fallen trees. No bushman would dream of sleeping under a tree that carried the silk bag of a processionary moth. A few species of birds, including cuckoos, eat the hairy caterpillers without harm.

When the caterpillars are ready to pupate they come out of the bag, march down the trunk, and in a procession search for a suitable piece of soil to bury themselves. Head to tail the grubs keep contact, by each touching its fellow, and also because they lay down a silk trail as they travel.

Sawfly larvae, called spitfires, also find safety in numbers. Most bushwalkers at some time or other have seen a mass of close-packed, squirming greasy-looking grubs which, when touched, rear up head and tail, then expel a yellow fluid from their mouths. Hence the name spitfire. The liquid is bitter, with a powerful eucalyptus odour. By night the groups break up and feed on leaves, often giving their gumtree homes a ragged appearance. By day the groups reform. When fully fed the spitfires march down the trunk and across the ground in a close-packed mass (instead of a procession). Progress is slow but eventually a suitable patch of soil is found and the grubs dig in. Papery pupal cases are formed, and the adults that emerge are called sawflies. Yet they are four-winged creatures related to wasps, and belong to the same order. The females have an egg-laying apparatus that consists of two tiny saws used to cut into leaves so that the eggs can be placed in safety.

Reptiles are also common and obvious in the woodlands. Brown snakes are the most dangerous of these. The increase in numbers with the spread of open grassland and savannah woodland may be caused by increase in the number of mice and other small animals on which these snakes feed.

Goannas have also held their own, and with increasing protection may become even more common. Best known and most widespread is the ground goanna. This lizard can grow to six feet, and is known for its habit of living in a ground burrow. At times, under stress of danger, ground goannas take to trees. Bushlore is full of instances where a frightened goanna has run up a standing man, mistaking him for a tree. This almost happened to me once in a central

56

Australian desert. A goanna we dug out of its resting hole headed for me. I kicked it aside and the goanna, disgruntled by a tree that lifted up its roots and kicked, headed for another tree and climbed it.

Ground goannas forage over considerable distances, up to a mile. A tremendous variety of food is eaten: centipedes, spiders, scorpions, wasps, grasshoppers, cockroaches, stick insects, beetles, moths, caperpillars, various insects, small mammals, birds and lizards.

Another well-known and widespread lizard is the bobtail or shingleback. Found in most open country as well as the woodlands, this skink lizard is not as slow-moving as it appears. It can scuttle out of danger with some speed. It is omnivorous, feeding on fungi, flowers, fruit, insects, and even small dead animals.

Birds of the woodland are many, both in numbers and species. Most obvious are the parrot family. One will serve to describe the group. The galah is possibly the most widespread of the family and is found from the inland through to coastal areas. The steady spread, since the arrival of the white man changed the habitats, is well documented in the *Handbook of Birds of Western Australia* by D. L. Serventy and H. M. Whittell. They point out that in the early days the galah did not come south of the mulga-eucalypt line, a transition plant zone in Western Australia. Most experts agree that the steady spread since then has been brought about by clearing of the country and so creating more grassland and open woodland—the favoured habitats of the galah. Another suggested reason is that there has been a slight increase in aridity, which has made more country suitable. By 1928 the galahs in Western Australia had moved south into the area near Mingenew in the northern wheatbelt. Then by 1950 they had penetrated deeply in the main wheatbelt areas. However, they do not penetrate into dry sclerophyll forest, and are scarce in the heavier woodland, favouring the more open country. A similar pattern has been recorded for South Australia and the eastern States; and today galahs are not an uncommon sight in Sydney suburbs.

Kookaburras also inhabit woodland country. In northern areas the bluewinged kookaburra replaces the laughing kookaburra. In the southwest corner and in Tasmania, which had no kookaburras prior to white settlement, some were introduced about 70 years ago, and have thrived.

With the drying out of Australia thousands of years ago, it is probable that many animal and some plant species died out in the southwest. Increasing rainfall once more created corridors of living space, both along the south coast and through the desert country to the north of the Nullarbor, but not every niche has been filled. The absence of tree ferns in the southwest wet forests, and the success of kookaburras, suggests that these two species possibly once lived there and died out. Similarly ice ages and wet conditions changed the pattern of life in Tasmania. Its cutting off as an island prevented the recolonization of some habitats. Both lyrebirds and kookaburras now thrive when introduced in these habitats.

The kookaburra is a giant among kingfishers. Though at times kookaburras still take fish, frogs and other water creatures, they survive strongly in woodland country; their food consists of insects, lizards, snakes and other small animals caught mainly on the ground, and sometimes in trees.

Territories of up to four acres are held, and research (by Veronica Parry) shows that not only are trees with nesting holes necessary to them, but also other trees as calling posts for defence of territory. Open country is needed for feeding.

The koala, almost a symbol for Australia, is found mainly in the dry sclerophyll and woodland forests of eastern Australia, or *was* found before too heavy hunting reduced its numbers. The koalas were swept out of existence in South Australia, almost exterminated in Victoria, and reduced to small numbers in New South Wales and Queensland. They are making a slow comeback—aided by restocking from island sanctuaries. They have also been bred successfully in Western Australia from animals in captivity, and it has been found that their food ranges over a far greater number of plants than previously thought; at least 50 species of eucalypt have now been recorded as edible to them, as well as angophoras, tea-trees, wattles, weeping willows, and even the buds of bottlebrush.

An interesting situation arose on various islands off the Victorian coast. At Quail Island in Westernport Bay a small group of koalas were liberated. Twelve years later the numbers had so increased that most of the food trees were destroyed, and many of the animals died. The position on French Island, documented by J. McNally, makes an instructive story. At this island, of about 41,000 acres, a small group of koalas were liberated at the beginning of the century. The animals thrived, and local people estimated that 5,000 were present about 30 years later. "Population crashes" then took place as the koalas ate out their food supply, the manna gum.

The few survivors increased as the defoliated trees recovered while the koala numbers were down. Today the excess stock is taken off to restock suitable areas on the mainland. When Dr McNally made his survey he removed 694 animals of the 1,000 living on the island. At this time the gums were again suffering severe defoliation, but the animals caught were all in good condition.

French Island is farmed, and so not a natural island. The farmers would have shot out predators such as wedgetail eagles, large owls, and probably goannas, which otherwise may have helped to keep the koala numbers in check. Bushfires, though destroying many koalas, may have destroyed the pattern of the forest also. So we do not have enough evidence from this to say that a natural island of 40,000 acres is not large enough to carry a koala community. A great deal has yet to be learned, even about the woodlands.

14
dark retreats
CAVE

Caves can vary from overhangs in sandstone, granite or other rock to huge tunnels and caverns running for hundreds of yards deep into the earth. As yet naturalists have only touched the fringe of knowledge of these places.

Shallow caves have been excavated by wind and weather in many kinds of rocks; and some huge caves are found in lava flows. The majority of caves, however, occur in limestone. Here chemical action (of water and carbon dioxide) has dissolved the rock to form tunnels and caverns. Changing conditions, such as the presence of more ventilation, reverse the process, producing a variety of structures—stalagmites (from the floor), stalactites (from the roof), shawls and helictites (spiral forms).

Every State has its caves.

Deep inside the conditions are constant: total darkness, high humidity, almost unchanging temperatures the whole year round, and little or no air movement. In some caves, particularly those of the Nullarbor, "cave breathing", caused by changes in air pressure outside, does produce air currents and slight seasonal changes.

In the darkness no green plants can develop, so the essential plant food base comes from debris washed in by floods, various kinds of fungi feeding on this debris, or material taken there by animals. (Interestingly enough the use of artificial lighting in caves has produced growths of higher plants such as algae and mosses.)

From the cave entrance, moving deeper into the cave there is a gradual loss of light. In the threshold area live some higher plants, and various animals. In the total darkness different animals may take over. Here we can recognize four groups: those that spend all their time in the darkness, on either the cave floor, walls, roof, or in cave pools; those that are part-time visitors, like bats, which sleep there by day and leave at night; the animals of the threshold zone; and the accidental visitors, which may be found anywhere in the cave system.

The animals of the overhangs and well-lit places include birds such as the rock warbler, sometimes known as the cavebird, whose nest is suspended from the roof. Kestrels, wagtails, and swallows also nest in shallow caves. Here too at night come owls and other predators to catch emerging bats.

In the threshold area the most obvious animal is the cave cricket or weta. Such crickets may appear in hundreds in the entrances to caves. In the day they can be seen shifting position, according to the amount of light.

Feeding on the plant debris and bat dung are many animals—springtails, slaters, caterpillars of moths, and various beetles; and preying on these are spiders, scorpions, wetas and other creatures.

Often animals that have become adapted to cave life have no eyes or skin pigment. The loss of colour may sometimes be a more immediate result of living in the dark. Some animals if returned to the light can develop colour. Many have evolved to the point where they are entirely white. Sight is of no value to permanent cave dwellers, and neither is colour. Ability to detect moving air is important, so touch is strongly developed, as in the long feelers of the crickets. Other animals hunt by sound or smell; certain bats, birds and insects have developed "echo-location" so that they can fly rapidly in the dark after food.

Grey swiftlets nest in North Queensland caves. Small half-cup nests are made of moss and other plant material cemented with saliva and glued to the walls. A clicking call may be linked with echo-location, but this has not yet been investigated.

Yet it is the bats that are the best-known cave-dwellers. In northern areas the large and striking ghost bat lives in both shallow and deeper caves. It flies out in search of victims—such as night-flying birds. A number of other bats are also found in caves. The bent-winged bat is one of the commonest; some caves may hold up to two hundred thousand of these.

A huge mass of bats congregated on a cave roof warms the air. This forms a natural "humidicrib", ideal for raising the young. The bent-winged bat is very widespread, ranging throughout the world, and like most species plays an important economic role by eating insects, many of which are harmful to crops. It has been estimated that the bats of Victoria eat a ton of insects each night. This is one important reason for the preservation of caves.

Some animals come to the caves to hunt the bats. Owls are threshold enemies, and carpet snakes prey here on bats. Feral cats, dingoes and foxes prowl in cave entrances. The Tasmanian devil and Tasmanian wolf use caves as lairs in which to eat food captured both outside and inside. The Nullarbor Caves have revealed that Aboriginal man not only used shallow caves as shelters, but penetrated deeply into the darkness.

A recent news report described how an exploring party in the caves of the Nullarbor found some fish swimming in the pools in the darkness. At the South Australia Museum these were identified as blind gudgeons. The fish were about two inches long, and yellowish white. Twenty years ago similar blind fish were discovered in wells in the Northwest Cape area. Gudgeons are usually small fish related to gobies, but have the ventral fins separate, instead of being joined together as in the gobies.

Many of the gudgeons are found in fresh water, and several records show they have at times fallen in showers of rain. These are no doubt fish swept up in powerful willy willies. Perhaps in this way they came to cave pools. Some of the fish coming down in showers of rain might fall into a cave entrance. Certainly they are tough fish. Over sixty years ago a parcel of gudgeons was sent from Wagga Wagga to Sydney by train. Twenty four hours passed and the fish were fairly dry. David G. Stead, seeing that the skin and fins were dry, decided to soak the fish in water before putting them into formalin as a preservative. Ten minutes later the fish had come to life, and began to swim round in the basin.

Gudgeons scoop up oddments from the mud, and also eat insects and other small creatures that fall into the underground pools. Though they lack eyesight, their other senses could be more acute than normal. Both by taste and by detecting water movements made by other small creatures the fish could find food.

15
the grey green sea
MALLEE AND BRIGALOW

Some habitats are so distinctive they have given their name to huge tracts of country. This has happened with mallee, where the northwestern section of Victoria is known as the Mallee District. The name can be used in a variety of ways. Mallee, besides applying to a district, or a distinctive complex of plants and animals, also indicates a habit of growth, from a characteristic root stock (as will later be described).

This remarkable woodland scrub occurs on limy or salty sandy soils, windblown sand, usually low lying country rising to about 500 feet above sea-level. Typical mallee country stretches from Western Australia in a broad belt eastwards to the border. The Nullarbor makes a break, but mallee develops strongly again in southern South Australia and extends in broad tracts to southwest New South Wales and northeast Victoria. Tongues occur in the midwest of New South Wales, and isolated patches are scattered throughout Victoria. There are small patches in southern Queensland and eastern New South Wales. Altogether it is an area of low rainfall, from 5 to 15 inches, mainly falling in winter—with a long dry summer.

This pattern of rather poor soils, low rainfall, and a long period of drought has produced an interesting range of plants and animals, evolved to solve problems posed by soil and climate.

Tough leaves, either rolled or hairy, or small, grow on many of the plants. Some hang their leaves vertically to cut down exposure to the heat of the sun. Some have no leaves. As a side effect, far more sunlight falls on the ground than would take place if the umbrella of branches were clothed in leaves. Many plants have long roots that can penetrate deeply into the soil and tap all available water. Some have succulent water-storing organs.

Mallee, though it may stretch for miles, is broken by patches of larger trees, salt-pans and freshwater claypans. These give variety to the landscape.

Two other plants, as tall as the dominant mallees, are found throughout southern Australia and also in the dry central desert country; one, the pittosporum or native willow, the other, very common along road edges where the extra run-off from the bare road surface allows a better growth, is the desert poplar or bell-fruit tree. The name poplar comes from the symmetrical habit of growth, bell-fruit from the shape of the fruits. The name "fire tree" is also used, since it grows after fire. It grows rapidly but topples in strong winds. "Horse-radish" tree refers to the taste of the leaves and twigs.

Ground flora varies with the soil—porcupine bush or spinifex on sandy soils and saltbush in the more saline areas. There is often a wealth of wildflowers, daisylike olearias, fringed myrtles, pop flowers, and the desert lovers called Eremophila (also called "emu bush").

"Mallee" has become part of the common name of many plants and animals. W. F. Blakely in his *Key to Eucalypts* lists 96 species of mallee among 605 listed eucalypts. These may be low shrubs of four feet, or trees up to forty feet. Their characteristic is a number of trunks of approximately equal size growing from a large woody root stock or lignotuber. Usually this woody lump lies buried in the soil, but often the upper surface is exposed by erosion. After clearing for agriculture, such twisted, gnarled and solid lumps of wood have passed into our language under the term "mallee roots". Many campfires and home kitchens have been warmed by the steady heat from a mallee root, though the age of home fires is drawing to a close. Most of the suitable mallee land has been cleared, and Governments are setting aside remaining stands as national parks or nature reserves.

C. A. Gardner, a noted botanist, regarded the root stock as an evolution caused by fire. Many eucalypts that grow to normal forest trees have a bulbous swelling just below ground level. They often send up a number of stems; one of these finally takes over as the tree trunk. Besides the eucalypts, tea-trees, sheoaks, grevilleas, hakeas, banksias and others belonging to the protea family have such woody sections, from the base of which grow the roots and, above ground, stems. An old mallee often shows all stages from termite-riddled branches killed by previous fires to more recent though taller dead trunks, and fresh and vigorous living trunks that have risen since the previous pruning by fire. Normal bushfires never destroy mallees.

Mallees are missing from the summer rainfall areas, so there may be some factor relating to the soil surface temperature that causes the mallee habit of growth.

J. Ros Garnet, in his *Vegetation of the Wyperfeld National Park*, which holds in safety a vast area of mallee country, describes how fresh water can be found even in the driest country by tapping the source held in the root system (not of course to be tried in a national park). By cutting two-or three-foot lengths of roots near the base of a mallee and standing these in an empty cup, a drink of good water can be gained, if these are left overnight.

Another feature of the mallees, important to the animals of this country, is the heavy flowering that occurs in good seasons. Many creatures come to feast on the nectar, mostly insects and birds. Some insects tunnel through the stems, so mallee can be a birth-place and a feeding place. In death the bodies become part of the litter on the ground, to be incorporated in the soil.

In season a profusion of wildflowers—correas, everlasting, fringe-myrtles and others—grow at ground level, to rival the splendour of the flowering mallee. Porcupine grass persists while winter rains bring up a rich assortment of plants. By late summer these die and leave the ground between the mallees bare. Below ground may be found two fungi that have created interest since earliest times. One, the stone-maker, is most commonly found in the mallee country; the other "blackfellow's bread" is more common in woodlands with larger trees but has been found in mallee.

Blackfellow's bread is a polyporus fungus. The larger fungi have a vegetative part below ground, which grows and stores energy perhaps over many years. When conditions are right the stored food is used in a prodigal outburst that pushes mushrooms or toadstools upwards almost overnight. The underground feeding threads mass into a huge lump of brownish material. This is said to have been used (when fresh) as bread by the Aborigines—though the story is doubtful. Certainly when ploughed up on farms the rounded masses do look like loaves of bread; some weigh almost 40 pounds. From a "slice of bread" kept in a warm place typical "pored" toadstools appear. I can find no record of fruiting bodies having been seen in nature.

The stone-making fungus, widespread, has feeding threads said to live in a close relationship with the roots of the mallee. This is called a symbiotic relationship, and is reasonably common in nature where fungal threads and feeding roots of plants intertwine to the benefit of both. With the stone maker, sand grains are bound into the structure and form "stones"—which may weigh up to twenty pounds. J. Ros Garnet mentions one at Wyperfeld Park which, when sectioned, showed layers of black material, perhaps a record of previous bushfires.

All fungi and small, often microscopic life help to recycle material for use by other forms. Another helper in the disintegration of dead plant material is the termite. Many species occur in mallee country. A close relative of the milk termite of the eastern coastal forests is found. In forest country this termite builds its home on living trees in the hardwood forests, and the workers forage over long distances. In the mallee the termite changes its mode of life, building a ground clay nest and feeding on the timber near by.

Flowering mallees have often provided a rich harvest of jewel beetles for the collector. The name "jewel" is apt, since the beautiful wings or entire bodies have been used in adornment. Not all the family, known as buprestids, are brilliant in appearance; but among the 800 species found in Australia there are enough to make the jewel name valid. A three-inch brown species is one of the largest, if not the most striking. Most of the grubs feed on the sapwood, tunnelling their way through the trunk. The larvae have small round heads and creamy white bodies. Feeding days over, the pupae rest safe in deep tunnels, to emerge, sometimes years later, as perfect beetles. These feed on the pollen and nectar of the flowers, then mate, lay eggs, and the cycle is complete. The adults die, fall to the ground, and once more become cycled into other forms of life.

Dr Barbara Main has discovered much fascination in spider behaviour. Among the group of spiders known as the mygalomorphs are the deadly funnelwebs and a number of trapdoor spiders. Most are dark-coloured, fairly large spiders, and all have fangs that move vertically downwards when the spider strides at its prey. In other spiders the fangs move sidways.

One trapdoor spider found in this mallee country uses its hardened abdomen to bar the tunnel—if the trapdoor is breached. I have tapped on this hardened abdomen with a pencil and tried to force a passage, but the barrier is effective.

Males and females build much the same burrows; for the mother it is home, nursery, and finally burial place. The females, and the immature males, have shortish legs ideally suited to the cramped burrow; but the male at maturity develops longer legs suited for a hunt over the surface for a mature female. Winter rains allow the males in this country to wander in search of mates. It is possible that a male joins with a number of females, and presumably does not long survive its nights of mating. The eggs laid in the burrow by the mother hatch and the youngsters emerge in midsummer, but do not leave the burrow until the first winter rains have made the ground soft enough for them to burrow.

Reptiles are common, though not confined to the mallee country. A large number hide in the leaf litter by day, to emerge at night in a hunt for food. Others, like the bobtails and blue-tongues, can be seen in daylight hours, except in the heat of summer—when most act as do those of the desert region.

There is a rich range of mammals and birds, and some have been given the name mallee as a prefix. One kangaroo is known as the mallee or blackfaced kangaroo. Until recently this was thought to be a variety of the grey kangaroo. There are two forms of this grey kangaroo, the eastern and the western, with an area of overlap in western Victoria and New South Wales. The western tends to be darker than the eastern, many almost being chocolate in colour. Eric Worrell told me he was able to recognize the species by the characteristic smell.

There are many other marsupials, as well as native rats and mice, since mallee country has a ground flora of grasses whose seeds provide food for hopping mice and other rodents. Grasshoppers and other insects are food for the carnivorous dunnarts. Similarly introduced pests like the rabbit and fox find the sandy soils a congenial home.

Birds abound, but since all habitats tend to merge and show variations from place to place there are no bird species that can be found only in the mallee, though many are typical of it. Dr D. L. Serventy made a survey of the birds of the mallee and the sand-plain heaths that go with them. He points out that the mallee belt is not continuous across southern Australia, being broken by the desert steppe of the Nullarbor Plain. However, a number of arid-land birds are found in both east and west, such as the mallee fowl, purple-crowned lorikeet, smoker parrot, mulga and blue-bonnet parrot, elegant grass parrot, southern scrub robin, chestnut quail-thrush, white-browed babbler, chestnut-tailed thornbill, Gilbert whistler, western whipbird, rufous tree-creeper, white-fronted honeyeater, purple-gaped honeyeater, yellow plumed honeyeater and the squeaker.

The most talked-of bird of the mallee country is the mallee fowl. Though not confined to the mallee, it has its stronghold there. The mallee fowl belongs to a group of birds that build natural incubators of leaves. Controlling the temperature of these nesting mounds is a complex task. Scientists of the C.S.I.R.O. have revealed an amazing story. The heat to keep the eggs round a vital ninety-two degrees is the natural warmth of decaying leaf litter and warmth from the sun.

Most of the work of nest building and nest care is carried out by the male. He digs the hole into which leaf litter and soil is scraped to make a mound about four feet high and twenty feet across. In the centre of the mound an egg-chamber is prepared and, when the temperature is right, the chamber is dug out and the first egg laid. By the end of a good season the female may lay as many as thirty-five eggs, at intervals of about five days. Each egg takes about seven weeks to hatch. The chick pushes its way through the soil, and once above ground takes to its heels and searches through the floor litter for food. This food is mainly seeds and insects, with fruits and flowers in season. The chick will never recognize its parents, and can fly a few hours after hatching.

The male bird during the hatching keeps the mound temperature round 92 degrees. The bird plunges its bill into the soil above the eggs, and tests the temperature either with the tongue or the skin lining the mouth. Should the mound be too warm, then soil is scraped away in the early morning, and cool soil scraped in from the slopes of the mound. Later in the season, with the summer dry, the eggs need the heat from the sun. The mound may be opened in the early morning for the warm sun to enter, and late in the afternoon warm soil is heaped up over the eggs.

This is no fixed pattern. Should conditions change on any particular day, the bird adjusts its behaviour to the needs. Opening and closing the mound, the male works through until the last of the eggs hatch, in autumn. Winter rains in the mallee once more moisten the leaf litter, and in early spring the whole story starts once more.

It has been suggested that the subtropical counterpart of the mallee is the brigalow country. Brigalow and the savannah woodlands were the main habitats invaded by prickly pear. In recent years much of the brigalow has been cleared for agriculture. It covers about twelve million acres of country stretching from Narrabri in New South Wales to Collinsville in Queensland, a section of country about 700 miles long (and about 450 miles inland from the coast). It has a moderately heavy rainfall, between 20 and 30 inches, mostly in the summer. The soils are mainly grey and brown clays, with some red loams. On these soils grow plant communities that vary from those that are completely brigalow, to brigalow associated with belah, yellowwood, gidgee, bauhinia, eucalypts and vine scrub. Brigalow is the Aboriginal name for an acacia called harpophylla (the name refers to the boomerang-shaped leaves). The misty blue grey of the foliage is the dominant feature of this country, the "national scrub" of Queensland. The trees are small and short-stemmed, and fork into a spread of branches. The leaves, or more strictly, phyllodes, have a steely blue look.

One interesting tree found in this country is the bottle tree. There are several "bottle trees" in Australia, the famous baobab or boab of northwest Australia, and the brachychitons of both the inland and coastal regions. The bottle tree of the brigalow is a slender bottle with a narrow neck carrying the crown of leaves. Though as timber the tree may be useless, it is a source of food and water for both man and stock. The ill-fated Ludwig Leichhardt found the young starch wood "tasty, and ... frequently chewed by our party".

When a tree is being cut down the cattle eagerly chew up the chips as these land. Sometimes only a cut is made, and the stock eat into the trunk.

Aborigines cut into the trunks, and the holes became a reservoir of sweet water. Even the roots make a food, being sweet and soft. The trunks were also used for canoe making, so here was a worthwhile tree to the first Australians.

DRY SCLEROPHYLL, *or open forest country, usually has trees up to one hundred feet high. This yellow ironbark in flower is typical of trees in a gum-tree forest of this kind. The hanging leaves, and their wider spacing, allow a great deal of light to reach the ground. Where the soil is poor, a floor cover of hard-leaved shrubs grows and provides the kind of "bush" usually thought of as being typically Australian.*

Woodlands and dry sclerophyll forest are the home of the brushtail possum. Darker varieties of possum are found in thicker forests, and brown and silvergrey varieties are common elsewhere. Though they feed mainly on leaves in trees, possums do spend some time on the ground, feeding on shrubs. The prehensile tail serves as a "fifth hand" when climbing. The brown stains on the chest are from the glands used by possums to mark their territory.

With its wealth of flowers at certain seasons of the year, dry sclerophyll forest attracts many nectar-feeding birds. This yellow-tufted honeyeater approaches its nest, built in the understorey of the forest. Honeyeating birds have a brushtipped tongue for sopping up nectar; at other times, when nectar is not available, these birds feed on insects. Australia is the home of honeyeaters, with about seventy species.

WOODLAND, *an open forest, has the appearance of an English parkland. Here woodland is seen at Dryandra, in Western Australia. Wandoos are the main eucalypt trees; but patches of sheoaks and mallee occur. At lower levels grow thickets of dryandra and "poison" plants, with smaller shrubs providing carpets of flowers in spring. The variety of height and form in the vegetation leads to an equal variety in the animals that live here.*

When mature, woodland forest shows many dead branches lying on the forest floor. These become food for termites and, when hollow, homes for ground animals. The numbat is one of the most striking, a marsupial that feeds almost entirely on termites, and finds shelter in hollow logs or dense thickets. Unusual among marsupials, it feeds entirely by day and shelters by night. If the woodland forests are preserved, the future of this beautiful marsupial is also secure.

The koala has its main home in the woodland and other open forest. Once it ranged over much of east and southeast Australia, but tremendous demands made by the fur trade, as well as increased fires with white settlement, reduced the once huge numbers to the remnants we find today. It will be many years before the open forests have many koalas, even with efforts to recolonize. An interesting fact is that the southwest corner of the continent has suitable woodland for koalas, but none live wild there.

The brown tree snake, here shown in its banded form, lives in open forests—in tree hollows and other crevices. At night it hunts for the small birds and mammals that are its food. One of the rear-fanged snakes, its venom, toxic to the small animals it eats, is not dangerous to man— though large snakes should be handled carefully. It ranges from the Kimberleys eastwards to the coast and south to mid-coastal New South Wales.

CAVES *provide a niche where humidity and temperature remain fairly constant the whole year round. Some animals that normally build sheltered nests, or use tree hollows or holes in the ground for shelter, find caves a ready-made home. This colony of bees has used the roof of a cave as a hive; with the comb hanging, the bees huddle in the open air. Such hives may last for many years.*

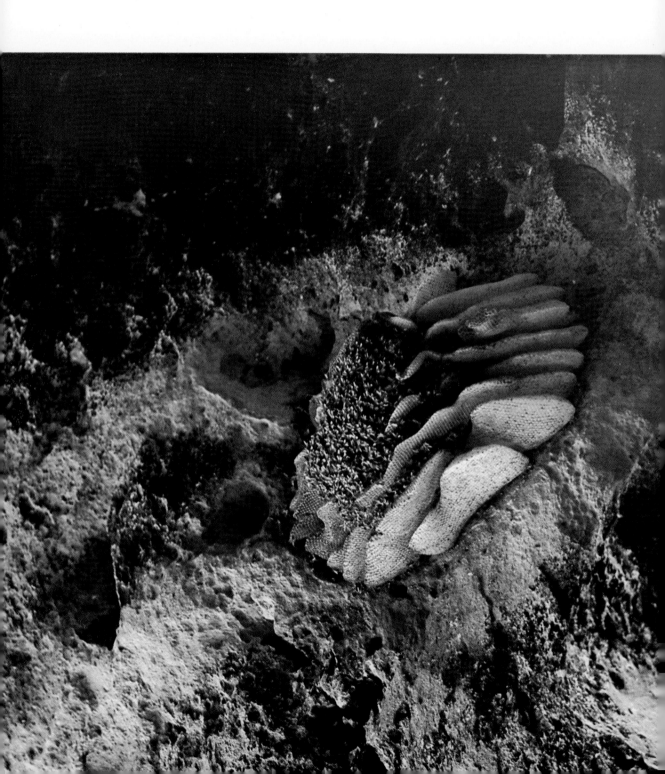

16
a temporary living place
CLAYPAN

These are a remarkable type of freshwater lake which may last for a few weeks or months, but rarely longer. Mostly the waters are brown and opaque, so the animal life is not obvious except by straining the water. In unusual flood years so much freshwater comes that the suspended mud is diluted. Then the teeming life is revealed. The problem arises: where do these animals go when for months or years the claypans are dry? The answer lies in the mud lining the depressions. A Norwegian scientist, Professor G. O. Sars, described many Australian species long before they were ever directly collected in Australia. He had sent to him packets of mud scraped from the beds of claypans. These were placed in freshwater aquaria. The interesting point is also that waterplants are usually absent from claypans. The animals must feed on organic debris which collects in the dry pans or washes in with the rain. They grow rapidly. Professor Baldwin Spencer described how shield shrimps reached a length of two and a half inches within fourteen days after rain fell in the pan.

Shield shrimps belong to the group of crustaceans known as the phyllopods—which means they are leaf-footed. They show the way life is geared to ephemeral pools. The eggs lie in the dry mud, perhaps for years. They may be carried on the feet of waterbirds, or strong winds may speed them across hundreds of miles in duststorms. With the coming of rain the eggs hatch and the tiny shield shrimp rows itself along with its many feet. From the shield projects the thin abdomen. Geology students will be struck by the resemblance to the ancient trilobites. In general the shrimps are handsome creatures, mainly greenish in colour. On the bottom they move in normal fashion, but near the surface swim upside down, perhaps so that they can watch from below where attacks by water beetles and other enemies may come. In good times the female shield shrimps can produce young without the males. However, there are always lean years in the desert, and then the males play their part. We have found, in temporary pools in Western Australia, the males and females in equal numbers. The eggs are laid on the water's edge, and will not hatch till they have had some drying out, a protection from disaster, for if the eggs hatched in a rapidly drying pool, the young would not have time to reach maturity.

A relative is the fairy shrimp, more like an ordinary shrimp though it lacks a carapace, and rows itself briskly along upside down with its many legs. America has a giant species nearly four inches long; ours are smaller.

A crustacean that seems almost like a transparent shellfish also lives in these temporary ponds. It belongs to a group known as Conchostraca or clam-shrimps.

Preying on all these are the dragon-fly larvae, water beetles and water bugs. Various ducks such as grey teal and mountain duck exploit such peels. Grebes and herons also feed here, and many other desert animals come to claypans for drinking water. Nomadic Aborigines found such temporary water useful, and would hunt near by for as long as the water lasted. Budgerigars and seed-eating birds follow the same pattern. When the water goes, they go.

17
channels of coolness
RIVER AND CREEK

Animals and plants of rivers and creeks face as many difficulties as those of coral reefs. There is tremendous variety in the speed of movement of the water, with raging torrents particularly on the east coast and Tasmania.

Inland rivers wind sluggishly most of the time, with occasional rushes after drought-breaking rains when soil, plants and animals may be swept with the torrent, perhaps to a new distribution hundreds of miles downstream. Sometimes the rivers shrink to small pools of still water.

There is variation between the edges, where the water is sluggish, and midstream where only the fastest swimmers can survive. Animals that have a floating planktonic stage are rare in such places. Many animals solve the problem for their young by taking more direct care of them. Others shelter under stones or make quick darts through the less sheltered waters. Some use the mud bottom of a creek in which to live, others prefer sand. The banks above and below water may provide burrows for animals. Trees not only hold the soil edge safe but keep the water cooler, and so more animals can survive summer heat.

With every flood the river bottom may change; a deep pool becomes shallower, a shallow place scoured to become a deep pool. In parts of the world where river fishing rights are important, active management improves running waters for fish such as trout or salmon. In Australia this kind of work has scarcely emerged, though there are some restrictions on the cutting of trees on river banks. In New South Wales river sheoaks are entirely protected, just as mangroves are in saltwater environments.

The food supply of animals in the stream is not necessarily dependent on plants either growing on the bottom or free-floating. Much food drops in, such as grasshoppers making a forced landing on the surface. Other animals fall from the trees. Yet there are water plants, varying from microscopic diatoms to giant river red gums.

Diatoms are microscopic plants with a "glass box" cover. The slimy surface on rocks in streams is often a diatomaceous ooze. Some idea of the rapidity with which these can grow is that a single diatom, given plenty of growing space and other requirements, within one year could produce 60 tons of descendants. Even after a diatom is dead its "glass box" resists decay, and often myriads of skeletons form deposits useful for industry. Diatomaceous earth is mined in lake beds in parts of Australia. It can be used in making polishing powders, and also as a holding agent for explosives so that they can be carried safely from place to place. Above all, living diatoms are a base of plant food for many microscopic and larger animals.

Although the central stream beds may lack larger plants, near the edges the first line of rooted plants includes bulrushes and sedges. Here too may grow some of the waterlilies, water hyacinths and others.

Just above the normal water level, yet flooded at regular intervals are such plants as lignum and cane grass. River sheoak, black box in the eastern inland, with coolabahs and other gums, grow on the river banks. European willows are a common sight on many streams today, acting as edge binders. Perhaps most picturesque of all plants is the river red gum, found over much of Australia on the banks of most inland rivers. Tea-trees are another attractive plant of river edges. The stately cadjeput, a majestic and tall tree, gives character particularly to the streams of northern Australia.

Most of these plants will also be found along lake edges, since running water environments merge into the still waters, and plants and animals may thrive in both.

At certain times of the year clouds of dancing midges are seen at river edges. Some water insects spend their larval lives clinging to the surface of rocks with suckers so that they can resist the tug of running water. As adults they fly over the surface. Among these are the true sandflies or "buffalo gnats"—not common in Australia. However, this country does have myriads of what are popularly called sandflies; these bloodsucking insects are well known on sea beaches, estuaries and also the banks of rivers and creeks. A great deal of research is being carried out on their life history to see how such pests can be controlled without damaging the environment.

Another interesting animal, the freshwater mussel, like its sea relatives among the bivalve molluscs, filters food out of the water; it moves slowly round the muddy stream bottoms. There are also freshwater snails and many crustaceans.

Various freshwater fish add character to the rivers and creeks. Best known is the Murray cod, a fine food fish. A 182-pounder has been caught; and given good conditions a three-foot fish may develop in about fifteen years. Murray cod were found first in the Murray-Darling river system and then in the Clarence and Richmond watershed, but introductions have increased the range considerably. Spawning seems to take place with water temperatures of round 20 deg. C., and a slight run-off of water into the area. This may be linked with the stimulus of water from summer rains or the melting of snow in the Alps. The cod eats a variety of food—smaller fish, freshwater crayfish, insects, and any aquatic animal of the right size.

Another well-known fish, the callop or yellowbelly, is found naturally in eastern rivers and creeks—and introductions have taken it as far as Western Australia, and to dams on many rural properties. Fish of between five to ten pounds spawn under the stimulus of floods.

The extraordinary lungfish is found naturally in the Mary and Burnett Rivers, and has been introduced to several more. Besides being a gill breather this fish can also breathe air into a "lung", a modified swim bladder. This means that when the rivers shrink with drought, the fish is able to survive where other species die. A full grown fish may be six feet long.

Tree frogs of various kinds are found in the trees and rushes of the river edge, and the tadpoles can flourish in creek backwaters. Reptiles such as freshwater tortoises are common, and as powerful swimmers can handle most streams.

Various lizards such as the water dragons and water goannas move from bank to stream. Birds are plentiful.

Many of the kingfishers catch small fish. Herons stalk along the edges to catch small prey, and active swimmers such as the little black and little pied cormorant and the larger darter hunt fish, from the river deeps to the shallow edges.

Water rats, active hunters of the stream, feed on mussels and other animals, and take shelter in hollows in the banks or in tangles of tree roots.

Most extraordinary of all animals, the platypus, lives in tunnels in the river banks. Usually in late afternoon the platypus comes out, to feed on yabbies, tadpoles, water insects and other small creatures. By late evening it retires to its burrow, though it may be out feeding in the early morning, and may be seen at other times of the day.

18
the great plain
SALTBUSH

Any traveller across Australia, by train, plane or road, becomes aware of vast stretches of open country, dominated by low shrubs or grass.

The Nullarbor Plain is the best known of these. This habitat extends well into northern South Australia and western New South Wales. Fingers of shrub steppe, as it is sometimes called, are also found interspersed with grasslands and savannahs.

Because of the size and interest of the Nullarbor this will be discussed in some detail, though the plants and animals are found over much wider areas. The Nullarbor Plain extends from the Great Australian Bight to at least a hundred miles north of the Trans-continental line, where the limestone disappears into sandridge country. The plain extends about two hundred miles on each side of the South Australian-West Australian border. It is mostly bare limestone or has a thin skin of soil. It is possible that a gradual drying of these plains, perhaps accompanied by fire, allowed massive sand movements, with the removal of this vital surface into the sand dune country to the north. Today, with a rainfall that can vary from two inches to seventeen, but on the average is only six inches in the central plain, a certain amount of vegetation has become established. In the depressions, called "dongas", where more soil can accumulate, larger shrubs and trees break the monotony of the treeless surface about them. On the sea edge, with heavy dews most nights of the year and a heavier rainfall, mallees and other trees grow. The Plain in its treeless form cuts the Eyre Highway only at one point. For most of the time the car traveller moves through a fairly heavily vegetated countryside.

The obvious plants of the region are the saltbushes and bluebushes. Both show characteristic adaptations to arid conditions, with succulent leaves and a hairy surface to cut down water loss through wind. Bluebushes tend to dominate the deeper soils where the rain penetrates. Saltbushes have a shallow root system and thrive in shallower soils—in the sense of water penetration. Also present is the "bindyi", a Bassia, with ferocious spines when seeding. Hence the name *bindyi*. All belong to the family known as chenopods or goosefoots, and some have already been described in the samphires of the salt marshes.

The common saltbush has a grey green look, with very salty leaves. One species, which may grow ten feet high, is the old man saltbush, often used outback for hedges. All make excellent feed for both domestic and native animals, particularly in drought times when the annual plants have been eaten out.

Bluebushes growing over much of the plain are almost the only shrub with the blue grey leaves their name implies.

All these plants are in a delicately balanced condition. Heavy grazing, first by stock, then by rabbits, has destroyed vast areas of this formation over the whole of southern and central Australia.

The dongas of the Plain have good stands of myall, an acacia often mistaken for mulga; the native willow or pittosporum; the false sandalwood, a myoporum; and a prickly acacia bush called the curara, sometimes known as the "dead finish" because when it dies, everything else is already dead.

The native willow, found right across southern Australia, is a graceful tree, and the fruits show a colouring that has led to another name, "native apricot".

After good rains there is an upsurge of annuals, including grasses. Hundreds of miles of the country become a sea of grass. I have driven all day over such plains with the air filled with birdsong, particularly of ground larks and songlarks.

With summer heat and drought, the grasses disappear, to leave bare ground between the shrubs and trees. With heavy grazing the salt-loving natives disappear; then the spiny bassias and nitrarias take over. Sometimes large scalds appear—areas of completely bare ground that remain so, for seeds are blown from the smooth surface. Only scarifying the ground and other erosion-treatment methods can restore such devastated landscapes.

The animal life of these plains is varied and interesting. Only a few animals can be mentioned. As discussed for dry sclerophyll, there are various kinds of land snails, adapted to the different kinds of country, from the wettest rainforests to the driest deserts. The Bothriembryon group is found mainly in the southwest corner, but a few species are more widespread to the east. One remarkably large snail is found on the western edge of the Nullarbor, and given the scientific name "dux". The animal has a thick limestone "door" to seal off the interior against long dry conditions. Besides this, the snail burrows deep into the cooler and moister layers of soil. Foxes dig out the snails, for these are big enough to make acceptable food. Perhaps even the early Aborigines found them savoury fare. After rain, when the animals emerge to feed on decaying vegetation, discarded "doors" litter the ground, particularly under the shrubs where the snails have been buried.

The most dramatic of the animals found on the Nullarbor is the hairynosed wombat—an inhabitant of the inland plains of Queensland from the west bank of the Murray across the southern coastal Nullarbor just reaching into Western Australia. One pioneer records that this wombat came to Western Australia at the same time as the rabbit. On the Nullarbor communal warrens are built and the entrances often radiate out from a huge crater with a limestone lip. Such holes in the ground may be ten feet across, though the normal burrow diameter is about two feet. The entrances of such craters break away and a person can walk in. As many as twenty burrows may join to make a community warren, and from the crater well-worn paths show where the animals go out to feed at night. However, wombats may be seen at the entrances in late afternoon or during the day in winter. Food is mainly grasses and shrubs, but wombats have been seen feeding on the sporeheads of ground moss. After rain some come onto bare areas, such as road surfaces, to drink; but for month-long periods they must rely on the water in their food, or on dew licked up in the early morning. The dewfall can be so heavy near the coast that the Aborigines were able to collect dew for a drink each morning by tying bundles of grass round their ankles to act as sponges.

Such heavy dews must also play a significant part in increasing the amount of water for plants in the soil near the coast and perhaps this explains why a corridor of taller vegetation fringes much of the edge of the Great Australian Bight.

The native marsupials and rodents suffered with the invasion of rabbits. Hard on the heels of the rabbits came foxes. Today the rabbit would be the commonest large animal of the Nullarbor. This also means that wedgetails, which prey largely on small mammals, also flourish. The occasional trees found in the dongas serve as nesting sites, but at times an eagle will build on the ground. For many years eagles have been harried as declared pests. Graziers feel they are a danger to lambing flocks, but most evidence from recent studies tends to show that this fear is unfounded. In good pastoral areas each pair of eagles occupies a territory of about 12 square miles, and this territory steadily increases in size as the country deteriorates. The test is how much food is available in the worst times.

In arid regions good rains may bring a temporary glut of grass-eating animals, ranging from grasshoppers to kangaroos; but for long-lived animals food must be present twelve months of the year, or else the animal must become nomadic or migratory.

All the feeding patterns so far observed show that rabbits are the main food of eagles. In the dry country, kangaroos and other marsupials, lizards, and birds become more important. Figures from the C.S.I.R.O. for arid areas give rabbits as 31 per cent of the diet, kangaroos 26 per cent, lambs 7 per cent, birds 15 per cent, lizards 18 per cent, foxes and domestic cats 3 per cent in terms of numbers of victims. The pattern is quite clear. Rabbits are the main prey, and the occasional lambs taken are a small price to pay for a predator that is hunting pest species most of the time. Since the eagle is a carrion feeder, many of the lambs taken could be animals that have already died.

It is to be hoped that regulations will soon be changed to allow full protection for this majestic bird, with its wing span of seven feet or more, that is such a feature of the arid country as it soars on thermals high in the sky.

It is interesting that Australia, which lacks the vultures and other specialized carrion feeders of Africa, has birds like the wedgetail and whistling eagles.

Equally prominent birds on the open plains are the songlarks and pipits. These are widespread in Australia in open country. On the ground, the pipit is an inconspicuous bird that runs rapidly in search of insects. The nest is built in a hollow, often near the shelter of a grass tussock. Disturbed, it flashes a tail pattern with the outer feathers white as the bird rises in alarm, reminiscent of the tail flash in many animals. Perhaps this is a quick warning to all others near by that something is wrong. In the nesting season pipits fill the sky with song as they rise in lark-like fashion. To many of us the pipit is known as the groundlark, and to children it is the grundy. Its strong bill allows it to catch heavy insects such as grasshoppers and crickets, making it a welcome visitor in the open paddocks of farms.

Also common across the plains are the brown and rufous songlarks. The male brown songlark has a black throat and dark underparts. Females and young birds lack this. Like the pipit, songlarks soar high into the air and pour out their melody. The song of the brown songlark has been described as like a rusty axle turning. This is the harsher tone; but it also has a call that can be characterized as "witchetty weedle". The rufous has a similar call, though lacking the grating sounds. When hundreds of these birds are singing on vast plains the effect is magnificent. Travelling across the Nullarbor Plains after a good season can be a grand experience when the larks and pipits are nesting.

At lower levels the shrubs and grasses shelter less obvious creatures. Reptiles of many kinds are common, including the bobtail lizard. Seen against the background of a cluster of red and black Sturt peas, its blue tongue, pink mouth and brownish scales provide an interesting colour pattern.

The vast saltbush plains will always have an attraction for those who have time to stand and look.

19
an endless aviary
GRASSLAND

The Australian Environment (see bibliography) has several sections on grasslands, one on tussock grassland formations, and another on hummock grasslands (dealt with here under desert areas).

Tussock grasslands have separate compact tussocks covering up to seventy per cent of the ground. There may be other small ground plants in good seasons. One huge tussock area covers the north of Australia from the Kimberley to Queensland across the famous Barkly Tableland and southwards into New South Wales. A summer rainfall of 15–28 inches fosters the famous Mitchell grass plains. Here grasses depend on the summer monsoons, and grow on heavy clay soils. In Victoria there were once similar tussock grasslands, but most have been cleared for farms.

Queensland Government botanist S. L. Everist, in a fascinating article on the famed Mitchell grass country, tells how the various species are confined to the clay soils, locally known as black soils, though mostly they are brown or grey. He divides the plants of this region into two groups—drought resisters and drought dodgers. The first stay above ground and fight to survive; the dodgers disappear, buried in bad times, and reappear when times are good.

Mitchell grass is a drought resister. Everist describes his investigations of this plant. It is a plant that has stiff stems and leaves. Just below ground are a number of short, scaly stems called rhizomes. From these, numerous roots spread out and down. Nearly three feet below the surface, fine rootlets appear, which may go down four feet into the soil. After rain, rootlets also appear near the surface, to feed until the ground dries once more. It is this wide-spreading pattern of rootlets that makes so many grasses successful. With Mitchell grass, Everist points out, a tussock six inches in diameter at the surface can have a root system thirty-six inches below the surface. The tussocks may cover only four per cent of the ground area, but six inches below the surface the roots range to 140 per cent. There is considerable overlap in the root system.

In this complex of roots, rhizomes and stems, starch is stored in good seasons, and seeds provide for new plants. With a light rain the stems may grow, but the rhizomes and roots hold their food stores. With heavy rains the whole plant can use up its food store in vigorous growth. Six or seven weeks later seeds appear, while more starch is being stored. Provided the plants are not heavily grazed by cattle in this period, they cannot be damaged by heavy grazing later, for the reserve starch is stored safe below ground.

Drought dodgers fall into two groups. Those that are annuals, like the flinders grasses and button grass, grow rapidly in summer, and in a few weeks produce seeds that fall to the ground to remain until the next wet. There are also annuals that grow after winter rains, and some, like the annual saltbush, grow at any time.

The other method of drought dodging is shown by the tar vine. This plant grows quickly after rain, sending branching stems over the surface. Flowers and seeds are quickly produced after a few months, then the plant dies back to the taproot. This root, stored with starch, remains alive for years waiting for the break in the season, while in the soil surface seeds of the vine also wait for the rains.

For the pastoralist these grasslands provide good grazing, with stocking rates of one sheep to anything from 4 to 12 acres, and cattle one to 40 acres.

The animal life is interesting and varied—but most spectacular are the grazing animals, whether kangaroos or seed-eating birds. The birds sweep in clouds across the sea of grass. These are the more obvious seed hunters. The seed, an embryo plant, is a rich food store. At ground level insects, particularly ants, are eager to rifle the treasure. So efficient are many ants in separating seeds from the chaff, that scientists have used them as unwitting agents in collecting seed needed for research purposes. When the ants have completed their above ground raiding, the scientists dig up their galleries and take the laboriously gained piles of seeds. In farming lands the attacks by ants on spread seeds can be serious.

A book written in the thirties by bush naturalist Henry G. Lamond, *An Aviary on the Plains*, brought to vivid life for town dwellers the drama of these inland seas of grass, the exhilaration of the open air and the drama when predators took their toll of the clouds of seed-eaters.

Plants form the base of the food source, whether as roots, stems, leaves, flowers, fruit or seeds. Then come the grazers of various kinds, from grasshoppers to budgerigars and kangaroos. The larger the plant-eating animal, the smaller its numbers. Insects appear in hundreds of millions; kangaroos only in thousands. On all these feed predators—hawks, eagles, dingoes, dunnarts. These are in still smaller numbers. Not that this means the hunters are stronger, or more intelligent, or higher, in any sense. The brave bulls are grass eaters, the powerful buffalo a feeder on plants, and birds like budgerigars seem to be more intelligent than cats or dogs.

The two most spectacular birds as far as the traveller is concerned are the galah and the bustard. Of the bustard the great naturalist John Gould wrote over a hundred years ago, "No Australian bird, except the emu, is so majestic". Unfortunately majesty and palatability here go together, and this problem bustards face the world over. Aboriginal man for thirty thousand years hunted the bustard with spears, throwing-sticks and traps of various kinds, for this bird, cooked on the coals of a campfire, makes a delicious meal. Later in the Aboriginal invasion came the dingo, a more efficient predator on bustards than the Tasmanian devil or tiger. Firing the grasslands as a hunting technique may have destroyed some of the birds; but the fire tended to produce still more grassland or savannah, so the plains turkey spread.

With the coming of the white man a more efficient enemy appeared. Captain Cook having tasted a bird on his voyage up the coast enthusiastically recorded: "We all agreed that this was the best bird we had eaten since we left England and in honour of it we called the inlet Bustard Bay." This indicates that the bustard was not only a bird of the grasslands but is, or was, found in other habitats.

Cook's bird weighed $17\frac{1}{2}$ pounds—a good average weight, though some have been shot at 32 pounds. Average males weigh about 16 pounds, and females 12 pounds. Yet bustards fly well, though there is a certain resemblance to an overloaded plane when the birds take off. In the air they are more attractive, but the slowness of lofting makes them easy targets for guns.

They have another habit that has often led to their destruction. Aborigines had taught them that a man on foot was a danger; but when the man was on horseback or in a vehicle the bird tended to be unaware of any danger. Since shooting such a bird is easy, very few escaped to learn caution from this new type of enemy. Soon the plains turkey became a rarity in settled areas. The slaughter went on, and States like Victoria lost these birds entirely. With a renewed interest in wildlife, an attempt is being made to restock Victoria with them. Unfortunately the bustard is a slow breeder, not becoming mature until four years of age. The mother lays one or two eggs on the ground and, if disturbed when the chick hatches, will slink off into the safety of the surrounding bush. The chick then squats tight and feigns death. Even if picked up,

72

MALLEE *shows a characteristic habit of growth, with a number of stems of equal size springing from a woody root stock. A fire may destroy the stems, leaving them as dead branches, but fresh stems grow from the unharmed "lignotuber". The charm of mallee country is seen best by those who walk through.*

Some trees that have only a single stem are common in mallee country. In cultivation this fuschia mallee becomes a small ornamental tree, but in the mallee country may grow as tall as eighteen feet, with masses of blossoms in late summer. The flowers are solitary, rich gold, on long stalks, and the fruit is quadrangular.

The most obvious animals of the mallee are birds and reptiles; but at night a host of small creatures appear. Often mistaken for house mice are the marsupial mice or dunnarts. This common dunnart differs from mice in its longer nose and more belligerent stance when cornered. Also it has many incisor teeth for killing small prey such as grasshoppers and moths. Like other marsupials, the female develops a pouch, which in the breeding season becomes crowded with young.

CLAYPANS *become a temporary living place for freshwater animals. Even desert sandhill country may have claypans, such as this flat between sand dunes of the Simpson Desert. Clay particles in the sand allow a growth of gidgee trees, and after good rains a number of shallow claypans develop. Shield shrimps and other small animals grow rapidly in the water; and birds and other hunting animals take advantage of the water supply. Aborigines once hunted on claypans while the water lasted, moving out when the claypan dried.*

RIVERS AND CREEKS *can be channels of coolness in a dry country. The Channel country of southwest Queensland is a maze of water-courses, and after heavy rains shows the pattern of creeks snaking round remnants of red sandhills that stand as islands. To the west the sandridges become more extensive, until finally they run for hundreds of miles. Even here in good seasons, rivers may flood between them and form long lakes.*

Water goannas live in creeks, rivers, and lagoons. The tail, flattened vertically, is used as a paddle. The nostrils on the tip of the snout have small skin flaps to close the air passages, so the reptile is well fitted to hunt in waterways. It is found across northern Australia, and feeds on fish and other animals. At times it falls victim to the blackheaded python, a snake that hunts in the same rivers.

SALTBUSH *on the Nullarbor Plain looks like grey-green sea. The name is used for all members of the "goosefoot" family, but some groups are also called bluebushes because of their slightly different colour. The most striking saltbush can grow to ten feet high, and is known as old man saltbush. It is often used as a hedge plant. All the saltbushes are worthwhile fodder, with a high percentage of edible material, especially valuable since they flourish on the salt country.*

GRASSLANDS *spread throughout Australia, much of them natural—such as this hummock grassland of spinifex growing on sandy soils in Western Australia. Scientifically known as Triodia, spinifex might better be called "porcupine grass" because of the sharp points on the leaf tips. Here the spiky leaves are almost hidden by the seeding heads. These seeds bring a variety of animals to feast—birds, mammals and ants. The spinifex leaves are also eaten by a wide variety of animals, and the clumps provide shelter by both day and night.*

it keeps its eyes tight shut and waits for release. One amazing instance was reported where a parent bird returned and picked up a baby, holding it between the feet, and flew off in triumph.

The courtship display is striking. The male spreads its tail, and this is fanned upwards and forwards to touch the head—which is bent backwards. Air is pumped into a sac on the neck. This distends the neck feathers until finally a great feathered ruff reaches to the ground. The wings are slightly dropped and the bird struts round calling loudly. The sonorous *whoooo* can be heard over long distances.

The main food is vegetable material such as fruits and seeds, but insects and other small animals are eaten. In grasshopper plagues literally thousands are eaten. One naturalist found in a bustard 150 caterpillars, and 50 ground beetles. All these were large insects. Another bird was known to swallow a mountain devil, a prickly meal.

Galahs, though needing trees for nesting, are able to range widely over the grasslands for seeds. The clearing of the forests throughout Australia has possibly caused the steady spread of these birds, once found only in the interior plains. Today flocks can be seen in the suburbs of Perth, Adelaide and Sydney. The rose pink and grey colouring make this one of the most beautiful of the cockatoos, especially in flight. Studies on the western grasslands of Queensland uncovered the following interesting feeding pattern: In the morning when the birds leave their overnight roost in river gums or any suitable tall tree, their crops are empty. At the end of a day's feeding a single bird may have 30,000 grass seeds in the crop. Since digestion starts immediately, a single bird may perhaps eat 60,000 seeds in a day. In this study the seeds were mainly of Mitchell grasses, Flinders grass, button grass and bindyi. On this basis a hundred galahs would eat about a thousand pounds of seeds a year.

No one has attempted to make any study of the number of galahs in Australia, but an observation along a flight line one mile wide found 50,000 galahs passing over. It could well be that the total numbers run into tens of millions.

In even greater numbers are the seed-eating budgerigars. I have seen flocks that I estimated at several million, with up to half a million birds on one large waterhole. Dead trees spring to vivid green life as thousands of birds land before drinking. Hawks take their toll, while the weaker birds that crawl into the grass around the water are later killed by crows—which gather round drinking places.

The birds spread out into smaller flocks for feeding, running swiftly over the ground in search of seeds. Every new watering spot means that they can extend their feeding range to places that could be visited only after thunderstorms had filled the normally dry claypans.

Trees are needed for nesting. Mulgas, sheoaks and eucalypts provide nesting holes, and may have dozens of nests, one in every suitable spot. Four to six white eggs are laid on the wood-dust in a hollow. The mother bird sits for eighteen days and is fed by her mate. Thirty days later the young take wing, and within four months have adult plumage. It has also been found that a young male can develop sperm within two months of leaving the nest, so favourable conditions can produce a "population explosion". This makes good the losses suffered in the dry periods.

Birds are not the only eaters of seeds. They have competitors among the mammals, particularly native rats and mice. Sometimes on the northern grasslands the longhaired rat appears in vast swarms. Literature records plagues in the 1869–70 years, in 1934, and again in 1967. Huge areas of up to fifty thousand square miles may be swarming with rats. Scientists setting traps for collecting purposes have caught a hundred in an hour. Densities of three hundred burrows to the acre have been recorded in Mitchell grass plains.

The rats dig short shallow burrows about eighteen inches long, and often with distinct runways between the grass tussocks. They turn to other food than the native grasses, attacking sorghum crops, vegetable gardens, lawns—and even eat boots and clothing. When these vast plagues develop the normal predators have little effect on the numbers. Wedgetail eagles and black kites in these plagues feed almost entirely on rats.

Besides the native rats and mice there is also the introduced house mouse from Europe, often called a field mouse. Regular plagues occur, and the actual weight of numbers tends to be overlooked. In one plague it was estimated that thirty six million mice were caught in several wheatgrowing areas of western Victoria. With 60,000 mice to the ton, this makes a weight of 600 tons caught in a few months.

So, on these vast natural and man-made grasslands, we see wild fluctuations in numbers of animals. Some are cloaked by the fact that the smaller mammals tend to feed mainly by night; but any traveller must be impressed by the huge flights of seed-eating finches, cockatoos and budgerigars.

20
a resource in drought
MULGA

Perhaps after the gum tree the best-known plant in Australia, at least in legend, is the mulga. "Heading for the mulga" is a way of describing a trip to the outback. This tree is found over vast areas of inland Australia. Even Victoria has a few stands, near the Murray River; and the other States have millions of acres. It grows in regions of both summer and winter rainfall, where rain may be as low as five inches a year or as high as seventeen.

True mulga is a wattle, *Acacia aneura,* which means "without nerves", though with a hand lens parallel veins can be seen on both sides of the leaf. The trees vary in height, from shrubs to thirty feet. The trunk is thin with a flaky slightly fissured bark, and a crown of grey green leaves. These leaves are usually two or three inches long, and very narrow—only one tenth of an inch wide. The flower spikes are about an inch long, and so is the pod. This is a very variable tree, and some broad-leaved forms occur. A number of other trees are also called mulga, or given names such as silver mulga, red mulga and the like.

"Mulga" is an Aboriginal word, first used by white men on McDouall Stuart's expeditions, when he was forced to do a lot of "scrub bashing".

It tends to grow on the better well-drained red soils, leaving the blacksoils to other trees such as gidgee; but even gravel ridges can carry mulga, though not so prolifically. In the sand dune ridges of the centre, it tends to occupy the troughs where the soil is more of a loam from clay particles washed in by occasional rains; the pure sand ridges are left to other shrubs and trees.

Though we can regard mulga as the dominant tree, there are numerous other acacias associated with this huge spread of country, such as gidgee. Sheoaks too occur in large stands. A remarkable tree associated with mulga in eastern Australia is the leopardwood. The darker outer bark peels off in small patches to give a beautiful spotted, "leopard" appearance. This tree starts off in a remarkable fashion, as a prickly bramble. No doubt this discourages grazing animals until, from the centre, grows a shoot that finally becomes the tree, and the bramble disappears. Leopardwoods are found in the hot plain country of New South Wales and Queensland, with relatives in the wetter forest of the coast.

As with the mallee, mulga lets a great deal of light to the ground. There can be a range of shrubs associated with the mulga, such as hakeas, dodoneas, cassias and others. Saltbush and wandarrie grasses may give a continuous plant layer; but where the rainfall is less, "spinifex" grass becomes evident.

The effect of aspect on growth is shown remarkably on some small Western Australian hills. On the south side, sheltered from the main heat of the sun, mulga flourishes. At the ridge spinifex takes over and covers the northern slope. The effect is almost as though a gardener had been at work, so exact is the division. Similar striking divisions can be seen on the west coast, where the white sands carry the true spinifex and the desert sands are covered with porcupine grass, the "spinifex" of the inland; and in coastal lands where soils carry tea-tree thickets and the sand, banksia groves.

A mulga tree, or mulga group of trees, is self perpetuating in a number of ways. Half of the rain that falls on the crown of the tree is channelled down the trunk, and so used entirely for the single tree. Leaf and seed fall helps to enrich the soil below. Running water near by may wash more soil into such protected areas, so the island of trees flourishes, with young seedlings growing up to fill the place of dead trees.

Because of the value of mulga as a stock food in drought times, lopping or pushing over of trees to feed starving sheep or cattle has meant the destruction of much mulga country. Normally a stand is not of great use to stock, since they cannot reach the leaves and must depend on seed fall and the grasses that grow under the trees. Some drought figures from Queensland are interesting. At Quilpie four men using front-end loaders kept 24,500 sheep and 350 cattle alive during a year of drought at a cost of 2 cents a head a week. A sheepowner on open Mitchell grass plains lacking this scrub would have paid about 17 cents a head a week in buying suitable fodder for this stock. Evidently if a station in good years protects its mulga stands from fire, and the seedlings from grazing, it will always have drought insurance in healthy stands of trees.

In the mulga zone we have a fascinating array of animal life. Not that in actual numbers or "biomass" it equals wetter lands, but rather in the more open country animals are more obvious. By night with a head torch more can be seen, as many shelter by day to avoid the heat. On cool days in winter, many animals usually regarded as night feeders may be seen in early morning or late afternoon, or sometimes throughout the day.

In arid areas termites have varied roles. Just as earthworms in moister lands process leaves and other plant material into soil, in dry country termites process dead wood and grass into soil, so unlocking a great deal. Yet in forest lands seventy to eighty per cent of damage to millable timber is done by termites, and only five per cent by fire. In arid lands where many termites feed on grass they can use up to half of the available grazing, obviously making them formidable competitors to all other grazers, from grasshoppers to kangaroos. They have many predators, but their main enemy is the ant. A weakened colony may finally be taken over by these aggressive insects.

It is interesting that termites, with nearly two thousand species, mainly in the tropics (about 180 species in Australia), manage to survive from wet forest to desert. The termite has little individual protection against drying out, but solves this by building air-conditioned cities. In colder areas the mounds may be below soil level—where temperatures are more stable. In warmer areas the mounds are built above ground, and some are gigantic, reaching twenty feet in height, with a weight of many tons. Interesting devices are used to keep the mound temperatures almost invariable, with as little change as one degree centigrade over the whole year. Some of the deeply fluted mounds, or the flat slabs of the compass termites, keep humidity and temperature correct by a refined air-circulating technique.

The recycling of nutrients into the soil is not necessarily true of mounds above the soil. At Atherton in Queensland, on land with 250 mounds to the acre, all the nutrients are held in the mounds. Since some mound-building colonies may live as long as fifty hears, the outcome from a soil point of view can be detrimental.

An interesting piece of work by two scientists of the C.S.I.R.O. Division of Entomology has shown that in good years some termite colonies increase. A particular species lives underground, and feeds on grass stems or mulga leaves, cutting these into short lengths and storing the food underground in chambers. When conditions are good the colonies create daughter colonies. As the grass and shrubs disappear, these colonies collapse, though some survive in the shelter of the mulga trees. Erosion both by wind and water reveals the old nests; these, being hard, do not allow water to penetrate easily, so the plants do not regenerate; and this, with fire, drought, cutting, and overgrazing by stock increases open areas. In dry times erosion is stepped up, with permanent degradation of the mulga habitat.

Research repeatedly shows how complex environment is, and how carefully we must work if we want to live with the country, rather than destroy it.

The broad pattern of trapdoor spider life as shown by Barbara Main has been described for the mallee country. Some other remarkable features are linked with the mulga zone—though not confined to it. A mulga tree or a sheoak tree tends to stand as an island surrounded by open spaces. Under the tree lies an accumulation of leaf litter of vital importance to some creatures of this dry country. It is a hiding and sheltering place for many small animals—but probably few as fascinating as some of the trapdoors. Dr Main has found that freshly hatched trapdoor spiders, offered a choice of littered and unlittered soil, will choose the ground covered by litter. Other species choose the open space.

Even the most overlooked and neglected of animals viewed through informed eyes can become a source of wonder. From forest to bare claypan we have a progression of moist to dry country. We also have a progression from numerous prey to rarer prey. Dr Main has found that trapdoors show a beautiful range of changed form and habits to fit into these varied habitats. To cut down water loss, apart from the burrow itself, some spiders in the drier parts have a much thicker and harder skin. Another change may tend to make prey capture easier. Those spiders in moist areas rest at the burrow mouth at night and seize victims as they come past. Beetles, ants and other creatures are captured. Those in bare places have eyes slightly larger and legs longer and thinner, so that they can see their victims better and run them down more easily. In the leaf litter, good eyesight would be of little help in seeing prey. Some spiders here fasten leaves of sheoaks or mulga as "trap warning lines". They rest on the twigs and the slightest quiver along one of these, sends them out in pursuit. The leaves may be six inches in length and give a much wider sensing area for these twiglining spiders.

The trapdoors themselves show changes in pattern. Those in the broad leaf litter of woodland are fragile with bits of litter attached for camouflage. Those in creek banks are of soil; and on the claypans are thick and cork-like to keep out the occasional floods. The twigliners use thin doors, also covered by litter, that can be flung aside easily as the owner races out after prey.

A beautiful example of a simple food chain is provided by the trapdoor spider under the mulga tree. On the leaves scale insects suck sap. To these insects come ants to feed on the scale's secretions—and a constant trail of ants pass up and down the tree. Lurking in the litter below, the twiglining trapdoors take their toll. In time the dead bodies of all will nourish the mulga. So the cycle is complete.

Despite their skill in camouflaging the burrow and lid, spiders do have enemies. Birds may see late hunting animals in the dim light of dawn. The old adage of the early bird getting the worm is not only a tribute to the early bird but a reflection on the worm for being out late. Bandicoots, scorpions and centipedes possibly find spiders in the dim light by the odour. Even smaller enemies can force the trapdoor despite the stoutest efforts of the owner, and some spiders have evolved safety devices. Some have side rooms, protected by doors. The most remarkable must be what Dr Main calls the "sock".

There is a layer or "sock" of silk, a kind of inner tube to the burrow. The top of the tube is loosely attached with a few strands of silk. Between the upper end of the sock and burrow wall, the spider pushes bits of debris from feeding. Should an enemy penetrate the door defence, the spider runs below the end of the sock, tugs at it and the tube collapses and brings down a load of debris as well. This seems like the bottom of the burrow, covered with fragments from old meals. The enemy, after scouting through the rubbish leaves the burrow. The owner can then adjust the sock and refasten the top to the side walls.

Perhaps we might close the insect story with one of the most remarkable inhabitants of the mulga flats, the honeypot ants or *yarrumpa* as they were known to the Arunta tribe of central Australia. Unlike the termites, which store food in galleries, or bees which store it in honeycomb, some of the workers among the honeypot ants are selected as the storage places. These are fed "honeydew" gathered by the others. The store grows larger and larger until the abdomen swells to the size of a grape—with a beautiful golden colour. The normal body armour is left as tiny plates on the stretched skin. The replete workers sit or lie or cling in

77

small chambers until needed by hungry workers. Each will give a drop of honey on demand, and takes a sip itself for its own needs. The nest opening is a small hole that runs sideways into the ground, then spirals downwards. A number of chambers to hold the replete ants may be developed, with up to twelve ants in each. The nest may be six feet deep or more.

This rich store of honey, in a land with few sweets, made the Aborigines keen to know honeypot ant behaviour, at least so far as finding a nest and digging it out. Mulga flats are the normal places, and this is no doubt associated with the ants' food supply. For some time there was doubt about where the ants find the honeydew. Normally it comes from scale insects of some kind, but these are not plentiful on mulgas. Naturalist Sir John Cleland found the answer. It has long been known that near the base of the mulga phyllode or perhaps half way along is a small nectar gland. Phyllodes are leaf stalks that have become adapted to serve as leaves. Most acacias are able to survive in dry conditions because they do not carry true leaves. An Aboriginal told Sir John that the phyllode is where the ants find their "honey". Sir John wrote: "If we got up early and looked at the young foliage of the mulga against the almost horizontal rays of the risen sun, we would see many glistening points of fluid".

It may well be that these glands, by attracting ants to wander over the tree, lead in the flowering season to the cross pollination of the flowers.

Reptiles are common in the mulga country; a number of lizards and snakes shelter in the litter by day, to come out hunting by night. One, the mulga snake, also called the king brown snake, and found too in wetter lands, is the largest of all our poisonous snakes. Eric Worrell writes though the maximum length is usually eight feet, he has some records of snakes that grew to nine feet. With the large size, goes a great amount of venom, and this also is a record for Australian snakes. Fortunately the venom is not tremendously potent, and some of Eric's native informants have said that only the largest are really dangerous.

Mulga snakes are not very timid; they tend to flatten their bodies to frighten off any approaching enemy. They are also snake eaters, and in captivity have swallowed common brown snakes. David Fleay found their tastes very wide, their diet ranging from bearded dragon lizards to birds, mammals and even lumps of raw fish or meat.

A striking reptile of the mulga is the largest of our goannas, the perentie, a fearsome-looking creature, though harmless to man. The dark brown back is balanced by an attractive reticulated pattern below. Normally these goannas live in burrows in rocky country and forage near by for food. Some grow to eight and a half feet, and weigh over twenty pounds. The head and neck are long and slender. The perentie when angered rears up stiffly on its powerful legs, and the skin under its neck is puffed out to make a fearsome display. Its food consists of snakes and other lizards. Some reports indicate that young kangaroos are sometimes killed and eaten. A bush camp soon becomes adopted by the local perentie, which scavenges for food. Like all Australian lizards it is not poisonous, though a blow from the tail can break the leg of a dog or knock a man off his feet.

A smaller goanna, the mulga monitor, is a tree climber, about a foot long. Widely distributed in central Australia, it lives in hollow mulga limbs and no doubt feeds well on the geckoes that share this habitat. Certainly in captivity it eats these lizards.

Birds of the mulga are typical of the arid-zone birds often referred to as the Eyrean. (Some are mentioned in the mallee section.) Two birds however have strong links with this mulga zone. The Bourke parrot, a small, rather soberly coloured bird, at close quarters shows a beautiful if restrained plumage. It has rose pink breast feathers, touches of blue on the shoulders, and its back is earth-brown—to fit in with the landscape. This parrot seems mainly a bird of the mulga country, and its nest usually is made in a hollow in a mulga or sheoak tree. The food is entirely seeds, those of mulga and other acacias and cassias, taken on the tree and on the ground below.

Another bird associated with the zone is the mulga parrot. The male is a most gorgeously plumaged creature, in greens, blues and red, with touches of yellow on forehead and shoulders. The female is duller coloured. Mulga parrots are found throughout most of semi-arid and arid Australia, especially in the mallee as well as the mulga zone and the central deserts. They feed on seeds and berries; but like many seed-eaters, are dependent on an available water supply. They will drink in the early morning and again in the afternoon (the Bourke parrot has a slightly different habit from most drinking birds: it will come to water at night as well as by day).

With many desert animals, even the more mobile creatures such as birds, prolonged droughts and high temperatures can cause extensive mortality. Professor Allen Keast tells how over vast areas of central Australia a heat wave with temperatures over 116 degrees for sixteen consecutive days in one area and above 100 degrees for two months in another created havoc with the bird life. 60,000 birds were found dead in one dam; and a 44-gallon petrol drum of water became filled with bodies in one afternoon.

Various mammals can normally live in dry conditions of the mulga country. Rodents called hopping mice belong to the Notomys group. These build elaborate burrows with at least three vertical shafts for escape. They remain safe in a stable environment during the day, and forage at night competing for seeds dropped to the ground. In good seasons their numbers increase rapidly; and by the headlights of cars hopping mice can be seen all around. By early morning the soil is criss-crossed with tracks. Research has shown that some species can survive with no free water at all. In captivity hopping mice have gained weight on a diet of mixed birdseed. One survival mechanism is their ability to get rid of waste nitrogen by means of highly concentrated urine. Many other animals of arid areas avoid overheating by the use of a deep burrow and night feeding.

The dominant marsupial of the inland country, the red kangaroo, rivals the grey in size, and is graceful in form and movement. A herd of red kangaroos in a zoo is a poor sight compared with the same animals bounding over a yellow, grassy plain or coming to a waterhole among the mulgas in the late afternoon. The males show the red colour that has brought them their common name; the females often have a smoky blue fur, and are known as blue fliers. At times females may also show a red colour. A large male can weigh 180 pounds. Females can breed at the age of eighteen months; but normally do not till about two and a half years. If conditions are bad this time may be extended—till five years old. In good seasons eighty per cent of the does have a young in the pouch, and about twenty per cent also have one at foot. Dry times change this—the pouch young die, and no more are born. Should conditions remain severe, death strikes among the adults. Some may move up to 120 miles in search of food. In the Northern Territory mulga scrub is preferred as a habitat. Only when the kangaroos have finished the grasses in this country do they move to the grassy plains. Short, green grasses are preferred to longer ones, and this is one reason why, after rains, kangaroos may congregate along roadsides for the "green pick" produced by run-off from the road surface. Only at such times do cattle and kangaroos really compete for the small amount of food available. In good seasons there is little competition, and usually grazing cattle improve conditions for the kangaroos.

Research elsewhere has shown similar patterns. With the coming of man and his flocks of sheep, much of the woodland as well as saltbush plains was changed to grassland more suited to kangaroos. As would be expected from their size, kangaroos and sheep eat about the same amount of grass, though the kangaroo converts fifty two per cent of this into meat compared with twenty seven per cent for sheep. Since the sheep grows faster, this difference levels out. Yet it is important to realize that the marsupials have evolved with the habitat and until the coming of the white man did not appear to be causing degradation of the grassland.

If one wants to get the feel of the outback, the heart of Australia, it is in the sight of a herd of red kangaroos bounding across the plains. And if the red kangaroo is the symbol of Australia, it is appropriate it should be sheltered by the mulga, a symbol of outback.

21
sandhills and stones
DESERT

This region, starting from the northwest coast, forms a vast ellipse that covers the central third of Australia. Over much of this country there has been no grazing. Once it carried a large population of Aborigines, the desert people, though most of them are now concentrated on missions or welfare stations.

It would be impossible to give more than a glimpse of the variety of climate, plants and animals of this vast region. High day temperatures contrast with night temperatures that drop below freezing in winter. Rainfall is erratic and may vary from twenty inches in good years to none in bad years. An average can be between five and ten inches, but averages tend to be meaningless in such country.

A fascinating diversity of life develops to grapple with changing conditions. A waterhole on a rock face shaded from the sun will provide a kind of lushness missing entirely from the exposed face. Deep canyons can produce an almost tropical look. A northward-facing hill slope may be covered with porcupine grass, and the southern side, having lower ground temperature, can sustain mulga. High rocks and road surfaces, with a slightly increased run-off, may produce slightly richer vegetation near by—as demonstrated clearly at Ayers Rock and along roadside gutters.

Some interesting survivals from wetter periods are the Livistona palms of Palm Valley and similar places in central Australia and also of favoured localities to the west and east. The cycads, also survivors of better times, provide striking plant associations in the MacDonnells and the deserts to the west. Grasstrees also are survivors.

A study by the Soil Conservation Service of New South Wales summarizes the position in the Centralian region of the desert. Eight soil types have been described, with their associated vegetation.

River flood plains have alluvial soils which vary from sand to clay; and, though trees may be scarce, ironwood, whitewood, supplejack, corkwood and gidgee are best known; mulga thickets and coolibahs grow—and on the ground many grasses and shrubs.

The stony hills and gibber plains have only a thin skin of soil, growing a few mulga or witchetty bushes and sparse spinifex.

The dune sands and the red sandy plains show an interesting pattern. On the sands, corkwood, mulga and desert poplar (Codonocarpus) are common, with a ground cover of spinifex. The depressions between sand dunes, often with a slight amount of clay, may carry stands of mulga and desert oaks. On the dune flanks grow spinifex and grasses as well as various acacias, with birdflowers in some places.

Better red loams give a green cover of mulga and gidgee, and similar stands develop on the yellow clays formed from run-off of the hills.

Some of the sands have a lime content, particularly in the southern sections, and here the copperburr or bassia may grow, as well as saltbushes and bluebushes.

MULGA *is a name given to a number of kinds of acacia, but true mulga is a narrow-leaved tree growing over vast areas of Australia. Sometimes mulga grows close, as a tall open-shrubland formation. With less rainfall, the shrubs become more spread out, and grasses flourish among the trees after rains. When dry times come, the ephemeral plants die, the seeds resting in the soil ready for the next good season. Long droughts may cause even the mulgas to die and, if over-grazing occurs, the young trees are unable to re-establish their shrubland formation.*

Mulga ants get their name because they use the leaves of the mulga tree or others found in the same locations as cover for their crater nests. Possibly the twigs and leaves help prevent sand from being blown into the nest, and also provide a slightly more humid environment round the nest entrance. The craters may serve as "dew traps" to divert dew and rain into the nest below, yet stop floods from pouring in.

Trapdoor spiders use mulga leaves and twigs to help capture prey. The trapdoor is camouflaged with small leaves, and longer pieces of twig are fastened to the burrow lip. At night the spider rests at the burrow entrance. An ant or other insect walking across the twigs shakes them slightly and the spider darts out and captures its victim. So its range of detection is widened by this ingenious device—a fan of twigs.

DESERTS *in Australia can vary enormously. This gigantic sandridge of the Simpson Desert is the closest approach to the conventional type of desert. Sandridges are a feature of central Australia, and they run in varying directions depending on the region. Basically they lie along a vast anti-clockwise swirl, with the eastern edge in the Simpson Desert running north and south; the southern edge in the Great Victoria Desert has east-west ridges. The tops of the dunes are of moving sand. The major part of the dune is more vegetated.*

A fascinating demarcation is shown on this desert hill. On the north-facing slope, where the sun shines all day, the heat-baked soil can grow only clumps of spinifex. The slight protection from heat on the southern slope allows mulgas to grow, giving a dividing line between trees and tussocks as clear as though planted by a gardener. Similar divisions can often be found caused by changes in soil types—and are a striking demonstration of how plant cover can vary.

Some deserts are stony. On this central desert the stones are called gibbers. These hard rocks once formed a continuous capping to the plains. With erosion the hard cap was broken, and, as a stony carpet, left lying on a base of clay. In bad seasons almost nothing survives, but after rain, plants appear between the gibbers. The stones are mainly of silica, which resists weathering.

HIGH COUNTRY *is a relative term, and Mount Kosciusko at 7,316 feet is not high by world standards, though the high country in eastern Australia does produce winter snowfields in southern areas. In the Kosciusko region particularly, a deep soil cover brings up a wealth of alpine flowers in midsummer. Above the treeline there are no gums, only smaller plants.*

Eucalypts flourish from lands of tropical heat to those of winter snow. Snowgums are a feature of the lower levels of the high country, and even in the depth of winter retain their leaves under a covering of snow. Some birds, such as gang gang cockatoos, come into the snowfields to feed on the seeds of the snowgum.

This diversity of plant life develops the same kinds of resistance to dry times as described for the grasslands. Growth after rains converts almost bare country into a carpet of flowers, with masses of everlastings of gay hues. The vivid scarlet of Sturt pea is sometimes in such huge sweeps that the eyes tire of its brilliance, and the acacias and birdflowers put on their gold and green blossoms.

The dominant plant of this vast desert region is the hummock grass, a Triodia normally called porcupine grass or spinifex (though it is not a true spinifex). The hummocks may be about three to five feet in diameter and up to two feet high. When covered with seeding heads, several feet are added to the height. In some species the hummocks are six feet high and twenty feet across. Others die in the centre, and grow outwards, forming a pattern of vigorous growing circumference and dead centre. Grasses and other plants may grow in the bare ground between the hummocks after good rains.

With overstocking, the coming of the rabbit, and long periods of drought, much of the plant cover has been destroyed, bringing a great deal of sand drift. Studies are now under way to plot the extent of the damage and see what can be done to check it.

The fantastic sand-ridge country extends over vast areas of the desert, starting from the northwest coast and sweeping south to the northern edge of the Nullarbor, eastwards to Lake Eyre and north to the vast Simpson Desert. Most of the ridges rise to about 40 feet, and some to 120 feet. These long ridges may run for many miles, lying mainly west and east in the western deserts. In the Simpson Desert the alignment is mainly north-northwest and south-southeast.

The sand deserts formed when Australia was passing through its great drying out, but would have been fairly firmly held by vegetation before the coming of the white man. Though it is forbidding at most times of the year, the Aborigines learned to live with this country, and explored it in better seasons when water lay in the depressions between the dunes.

It is impossible for a white man to appreciate the depth of pragmatic knowlege the Aborigines had of their country. Take for example the selecting of roots of an acacia to be used as spears, in country where trees had trunks too short above ground to be used for this. A man would not only look for a tree of the right age, but would walk round the plant, breaking off branchlets until he found the side where the leaves were the least brittle. This was the best watered side. Fine hair cracks on the ground indicated where the roots lay, and some patient digging could bare a suitable length of root.

Other plants were known for their water-holding roots. A length of desert kurrajong or eucalypt root was stood in a water holder until enough water dripped out to provide a life-saving drink.

One of the striking trees of the desert country, with bright green foliage and bellshaped fruits, is the desert poplar, sometimes called horseradish or fire tree, since it grows vigorously after fire, sending up a long, spindly trunk. This is favoured by wood-boring grubs, until it topples in the first strong wind. Sturdier and longer lasting is the desert oak, a casuarina well-fitted to its environment. This genus of trees has a representative in the beach sheoak of the coral cays, and in the river oak of freshwater streams, where it is protected by law as an efficient soil binder.

For dry conditions the trees have reduced the true leaves to mere scales, and the food producing is taken over by the stems. A sharp tug on one of these "leaves" and the tiny "king's crown" of scales shows that each scale spike is a true leaf. In most species the sexes are separate trees. When the male tree is in flower the red blossoms make it appear as though dying. The deeper set female flowers glow red when struck by sunlight. The name casuarina was given because of the resemblance of the drooping branches to the wiry feathers of the cassowary. The desert oak has another defence against drying out—a thick corky bark. In bad times up to ninety per cent of the branchlets may be dropped, giving a threadbare appearance. In good times it becomes thickly foliaged, and because of its height and shapeliness is one of the outstanding sights. Occasional extensive groves appear.

The inland spinifex is a prickly niche offering shelter for an interesting group of animals. The rounded clump is an intertwined mass of spear-like leaves with, in season, dozens of seeding plumes. The sharp needles prevent larger enemies from pursuing the inhabitants of the clump. The mass of leaves means that wind speeds are slowed until, in the heart of the clump, the air is relatively still. This lowers the temperature and, more important, the humidity can remain higher. The leaf litter on the ground may retain enough moisture to allow feeding and even breeding. Dr H. Bustard records that in a study in central Australia where no significant rain had fallen for about twelve years the mulga had died over large areas and the spinifex also seemed dead. Yet inside the clumps was a wealth of life. Cockroaches, the main inhabitants, can survive by eating the leaf litter. Spiders are also common, possibly through eating some of the cockroaches. At the top of the food pyramid are the porcupine bush geckos.

In better times the same bushes carry many more animals, such as grasshoppers, centipedes, other geckoes and legless lizards. Dr Bustard tells how he saw porcupine bush geckoes attacked by one of the legless lizards, which are their major enemies. This particular gecko exudes a black fluid from its tail. I have tasted this, and it has no perceptible effect, but it certainly worries lizard enemies. The liquid cannot be squirted, as with the spinytailed geckoes, but the tail is wiped on the enemy's face and this causes the attacker to release the victim.

So life in a porcupine bush has its hidden dramas, rarely seen by people busy avoiding the spears.

In these spinifex grasslands live huge colonies of termites. One has the scientific name of *triodiae* because it feeds on the spinifex, though it also eats other grasses, which it stores in its huge mounds. These are among the largest mounds built by any termite in Australia, and may be more than twenty feet high, with flying buttresses projecting from the tall central structure. Early explorers coasting along the west side of the continent called them "kaffir huts" because they took them to be the homes of the Aborigines. Such a mound can shelter many hundreds of thousands of termites. Some are known to have been occupied for over fifty years, but whether old mounds are recolonized or the queens of this particular species are longlived, is not yet known. The workers gather the grass stalks by building underground tunnels for hundreds of yards round the nest. Sometimes these can be lifted from the sandy surface without breaking; they are a feature of the ground between tussocks.

The nesting mounds make favoured air-conditioned homes for many animals, and at least one interesting food relationship has developed. The termites eat the grass stems of the spinifex, so this is the base of the food pyramid. From this harvest of grass stems hundreds of thousands of termites flourish in each mound. Here too are hundreds of termite geckoes, which appear to eat only these insects. Here also lives a dwarf python that appears to feed entirely on geckoes. It is the apex of this food pyramid.

For people used to the sombre cockroaches of the suburbs, the desert ones are striking. One species is a brilliant green with a broken line of yellow along the edge of the body. Perhaps safe from most enemies by the flaunting of its warning colours, it is easily captured since it does not beat a hasty retreat to the prickly ramparts of the spinifex, as do most other small animals of these hummock grasslands.

It might seem that the desert would be too harsh a place for survival for animals such as frogs, yet when rains do fall the frogs are able to take in water rapidly. Perhaps the most famous is the waterholding frog. Some of the descriptions by early explorers are interesting. Baldwin Spencer, a zoologist whose name became associated with studies in the red centre, told how the ground was so hard it had to be chipped away. When one side of the burrow was opened the frog remained perfectly still; its lower eyelid was drawn up over the eye and was very opaque, giving rise to the belief among the blacks that the frog is blind. In the sunlight after a short time it opened its eyes. With the body cut open, a certain amount of water was seen in the subcutaneous spaces, but even more water, which caused the great swelling out of the body, was contained in the body cavity itself. Other explorers told how the Aborigines, on digging up the frog, would squeeze out the water to get a welcome drink, then take the body to camp for a meal. So, the frog solved the long periods without rain.

Some remarkable devices to defeat the harshness of desert life have been developed by reptiles. Dr Bustard tells how velvet geckoes survive. The marbled velvet gecko is common throughout much of Australia, with a related species in the northeast. The gecko hides under the bark of dead trees, and in rock crevices. As with many desert animals, mammals as well as reptiles, the geckoes have fattened tails. These are food stores, from where the fat can be used in bad times. Dr Bustard records that after complete starvation for six months the body weight of a gecko dropped only by one fifth. Another scientist found that this velvet gecko could survive for six months without food or water, and for a year on water alone. It is probable that the water needed, when it is not in the food supply, can be obtained from the oxidation of stored fat.

Dr Bustard mentions one velvet gecko that lives in empty trapdoor spider burrows.

The fattened tail is used as a door, making a seal that keeps the burrow at the correct humidity by cutting down water loss. It also keeps the temperature much lower than on the surface. The lizard creeps as far down the burrow as it is possible to go, then uses its tail as a plug. This tail, mostly fat, is a very poor conductor of heat. So the water lost from the lungs is trapped in this underground chamber and the reptile creates a suitable microclimate where it can survive.

Death adders are found over much of Australia. The desert form is yellowish to brick red, compared with the dirty grey of more coastal forms. In winter the adder may hunt by day; in summer it waits till the comparative cool of night to go in search of victims. The "spine" on the tail is apparently used as a bait; the death adder wriggles the tail tip. Some luckless lizard or bird investigating this likely bit of food becomes food for the adder.

Perhaps the lizard best known to most travellers in the desert is the mountain or thorny devil. This spiky dragon feeds on ants, small black ones that form trails; so the devil can station itself and lick them up one at a time, with perhaps 5,000 ants eaten at one meal. Many lizards feed on ants, for these insects are among the commonest desert animals.

Thorny devils are hatched from eggs laid in a burrow dug in the soil, become mature at three years of age, and may live for about twenty years. There has been a lot of argument about their drinking habits. In captivity they will lap up water with the tongue; and many books describe their ability to absorb water through the skin—though this is doubtful. Recent observations seem to show that if a devil puts one foot in water the fluid passes along the skin to the mouth and is swallowed. I am puzzled why the lizard could not just drink the water, though possibly in light showers the total wetting of the body might allow it to drink in this fashion.

Bird life of the desert is as varied as for any other habitat, with seed-eaters plentiful. Finches and pigeons are common, and among these are the crested bronzewing and the flock pigeon, which shows huge fluctuations in numbers. The last few years have seen vast flocks, particularly on the northern grasslands. Crested pigeons always appear to hold their numbers in arid regions, and seem to be spreading their range nearer the coast. The plumed pigeons common in spinifex country, particularly along the rock ridges, are among the most attractive of birds. All these species are well fitted with rather hard bills for hammering at seeds. At times they will also feed on insects, including termites and caterpillars.

The spinifex-bird builds its nest in a spinifex hummock, and feeds mainly on the ground in this type of country. Its song is something like that of the pipit, and has been characterized as "je suis a vous".

Perhaps we can close the story of desert birds with a short account of the will o' the wisp, the night parrot. It was seen by early explorers, and the first specimen was probably collected in the western desert in 1854. Occasional birds were collected later, but only one has been taken in this century. A number of sightings have been reported, though there has been no certain identification in the last twenty years. I have a very good account, from the western desert, that appears to be of the long lost night parrot. Its general colour is a yellowish green, and it looks something like the ground parrot. Most sightings are in spinifex country, and why its numbers have declined is something of a puzzle. Predation by foxes and feral cats has been blamed, but since vast areas of its habitat are unchanged and feral cats at least were present when it was abundant, there must be some other reason. It would be rash to claim it is extinct. While the habitat remains largely unchanged, it is likely that the animals that live there survive.

In droughts birds suffer huge losses. At first, species do not breed or else lay reduced clutches. Should a drought persist, catastrophic losses take place. When good times come the birds not only may have larger clutches but may breed several times in succession. This is paralleled by mammals like the dunnart and house mice. Plagues that develop appear to do so soon after good rains fall following prolonged drought.

Nature, taking the marsupial form and having little else to work on in this island, evolved a host of forms similar to those of other continents. We have the spiky echidna, an egg-laying mammal resembling the porcupines of other lands; the hopping marsupials, similar to the hopping rodents; the monkey-like cuscus, and, in the sandhill country of the desert, the marsupial mole, very similar to the desert mole of Africa.

Though the marsupial mole is only about six inches long, its golden silk fur made it an attractive ornament for the desert Aborigines. A horny shield covers the face, and no eyes are visible. Very little is known about this tiny creature, but it *is* known to feed on earthworms in captivity. In the desert sandridges it could feed on various insect larvae; and though usually said to be found only in the western desert, there is a very good description of the animal from the Simpson Desert in the east. It has been described here as living in colonies six to eight inches underground. The tell-tale hillocks show where the colonies exist. They are said to have a strong smell. In the west a mole was seen above ground in broad daylight wriggling in snake-like fashion over the sand. It made a triple track and disappeared into the sand leaving a tiny depression about an inch across.

When this animal becomes better known it should provide a fascinating story. Living as it does in desert sandhills, it must be magnificently adapted to survive without water. It is reported to appear above ground after thunderstorms, so no doubt licks up some water in these occasional downpours.

There are other flesh-eating animals in the desert. The long-tailed dunnart and the slightly larger mulgara represent (at the smaller end of the scale) the range of marsupial carnivores that pass in size through the native cats, to the tiger cats, the Tasmanian devils and finally to the Tasmanian tiger.

The mulgara is one of the best known of the hunters of the desert country. Feeding on insects, scorpions, centipedes, spiders, lizards, snakes, small mammals and birds, the mulgara is a successful animal. When eating a mouse the mulgara kills it with a single bite in the back of the head. A naturalist keeping this animal in captivity found that if given skinned mice, it made a messy job of eating, apparently needing the lay of the fur to know which way to begin its feeding. Snakes were killed by biting, shaking, and repeating this until the reptile was slow enough to be killed by a bite behind the head. Scorpions and spiders were treated the same way, and this parallels the "scrabbling", patting with the feet, used by bandicoots when handling prey that might bite or sting.

Recent research has shown that the mulgara can survive without drinking water, by staying in burrows in the heat of the day. Its food provides the water needed, and since a mulgara eats about a quarter of its own body weight every day, there arises the problem of how to get rid of urea, the waste product from eating protein. With most mammals this is where a great deal of water must be lost, since the urea is excreted in urine. Desert animals like the mulgara have very efficient kidneys that can excrete urine in highly concentrated form.

The desert country holds some native cats but no larger marsupial carnivore. Dingoes are common. The dingo is a variety of the domestic dog, and has done well in most parts of Australia, though the more recent introduction of the fox has provided an effective competitor in the hunt for small animals.

Another flesheater is the dalgite, or bilby, or rabbit-eared bandicoot. Once widespread, its stronghold today is the desert lands. It is an incredibly fast burrower, and in the desert the burrows may be six feet deep, and made in a spiral. Here the dalgite shelters from heat and dryness during the day, coming out at night to look for food such as beetles, insects and other small animals. In places the main food appears to be termites. The coastal dalgite is a larger species, and today very rare.

Rock wallabies are a common sight in rocky outcrops of the arid centre. On cool winter days they may be seen at any time, and even in high summer in the late afternoon these animals appear from the rock crevices where they have been sheltering. Dr T. Ealey, when studying the euro in such rock outcrops, found that though outside temperatures might vary from 65 degrees to 115 deg F., inside rock clefts the temperature remained fairly stable, not quite so much as in deep caves but ranging from 80 to 90 degrees.

So the need to keep body temperatures stable is solved by living in a constant environment during the heat of day. Moving round the rocks the wallabies show the same surefooted ability as goats, their feet having roughened pads to grip the rock surface. The tail is relatively long, and has a hair tuft. No doubt as with the tree kangaroos the tail, functioning as a balance, also helps in movement up steep rock surfaces. At night the rock-wallabies may graze considerable distances from their home caves. The commonest is the brushtailed rock wallaby found over most of Australia. The gaily coloured ringtailed rock wallaby ranges in the eastern desert lands from South Australia through to south-west Queensland.

Much pioneering work on the problem of desert survival was done by scientists Knut and Bodil Schmidt-Nielsen. In a study of the desert rat of America they found that no water was stored in special tissues to stave off the effects of long dry periods. About 65 per cent of the body weight was water and this percentage remained the same through both wet and dry seasons. After being fed on dried barley for eight weeks the animals gained weight. The only possible way to obtain the water needed was to oxidize the food. Water consisting of hydrogen and oxygen can be obtained by oxidizing hydrogen in the food. Dry barley gives 54 per cent of water when oxidized in this way. That solves the problem of getting the water. How does the animal cut down on water loss? People and many animals keep their body temperatures stable by sweating. Desert rats have reduced all sweat glands except some on the toe pads. However, a small amount is lost through the skin and a large amount through the lungs. This means that in dry desert air desert rats would die in spite of all their body processes. By day the desert rat lives in its deep burrow, where temperatures remain comparatively low and humidity comparatively high. Only the chill of night, by reducing the likelihood of gaining heat from the air and also by raising the humidity to acceptable levels, allows the rodent its chance to feed. In the burrows the temperature in summer ranges from 75 to 88 degrees and the humidity from 30 to 50 per cent. On the surface the relative humidity during the day can drop to less than ten per cent but by night it ranges from 15 to 40 per cent with a temperature range of 60 to 75 degrees. This is a tolerable set of conditions for the rat. The final problem is excretion of nitrogen. Man can tolerate levels of only 6 per cent urea in his urine. The desert rat has such efficient kidneys it can concentrate urea to a level of 24 per cent. In terms of salts it is twice as salty as seawater. It was found that if the rat was forced to drink sea water it could thrive on it.

The long neck of the camel has made it an efficient desert grazer, for it can reach and pull down the highest branches of the mulga. In certain areas today it has become a pest, fouling watering troughs and breaking fences. Some of the Aboriginal tribes have taken to camels as a means of transport.

The Schmidt-Nielsens found that camels solve overheating problems by allowing blood temperatures to rise to about 104 degrees during the day, then at night to cool down to 95 degrees—instead of keeping the blood stable at round 98 degrees as people do. To stop the blood temperature from rising too high the animal sweats. Where the camel has plenty of water the sweating rate is increased and the body temperatures kept constant. In hot sun the camel sits facing the sun to cut down the amount of sunlight absorbed. The fur on the back is thicker, and this serves as an insulator to keep heat out. Shorn camels need more water than unshorn ones. Camels lose water by sweating, and also for normal bodily needs they must drink. After a two weeks' desert trek a camel becomes emaciated, both from using up its fat store and from water loss. It can drink as much as thirty gallons of water in ten minutes.

22
above the snow-line
HIGH COUNTRY

We have seen how on a journey from the ocean to the red centre we normally pass through stunted vegetation along the coastal edge and then denser and more luxuriant vegetation where good soil, high regular rainfall and shelter allow forests to develop. With increasing distance from the coast the tree heights dwindle until in the arid centre, except in favoured localities, we are once more among widely spaced grass tussocks, similar to those of the dune zones.

A much shorter path from lush to sparse can be taken on a journey to the high country, where finally one emerges on windswept moors covered only by low herbs and low shrubs.

Yet again in this high country a variety of habitats does occur—grasslands, low heaths, herb fields, peat swamps, bogs, creeks and lakes.

Dr A. B. Costin defined the high mountain country as that of the lower limits of winter snowline. This varies with latitude, from 5,500 to 5,000 feet in the Australian Capital Territory and New South Wales, 4,500 feet in southern Victoria, and 3,000 feet in Tasmania. Aspect can also play a part in the height of the winter snowline. There are about 1,000 square miles of snow country in New South Wales, 870 in Victoria, and 2,500 square miles in Tasmania.

In these lands there is winter snow for at least one month of the year, though normally up to four months the ground is under snow. Some small areas may carry snow the whole year round in cool summers.

Dr Costin points out that the Australian Alps are in the nature of soil mountains where there are often many feet of soil on the parent rocks, and the gentle slopes tend to allow a good development.

The Tasmanian snow country is more like that of its British counterparts, with little soil development. It is basically a large rocky central plateau with a smaller one in the northwest.

Daily temperature fluctuations of 50 degrees, causing "frost heaves", high intensity summer storms and the deep soils themselves make these areas very vulnerable to erosion. Dr Costin stresses the need for great care in land use, a warning that unfortunately has come too late to save many lands.

What are the problems facing plant and animal life in this high country? Obviously the presence of snow is one factor. Others are high winds, and heavy rainfall with the paradox of lack of water where thin soils fail to hold rain. Rapid temperature fluctuations with high summer heat can cause drying out. There is too the rapidly eroding soil.

Many adaptations have developed among plants that survive in this region. Dwarfing, seen in woody plants, is the most obvious since this cuts down the effect of wind. Some plants become cushions, with their new shoots growing in the protection of parent branches. Small, spiky, hairy or rolled leaves all help in cutting down water loss. Strong root developments help anchor the plants against the tear of wind and water. On the more exposed rocks only the lichens and mosses survive. With some protection, more plants develop, to give the high country a fascinating aspect in summer. Only the western heaths can equal the floral show in a good season.

There is not only a wealth of wildflowers, but differences in foliage, and bright berries. Though the climate and other conditions are severe there is a rich variety of plants, and these are shared between all the high country lands.

Botanist Thistle Harris points out that in the high moors there is a range of plant families, a suite different from the dominant ones of the rest of Australia. Orchids, buttercups, snapdragons, the parsley family, gentians and the rose family are abundant, but acacias, pea flowers, myrtles, proteaceae and mintbushes have few species in these lands.

Two families, the heaths and the composites, are features both of alpine lands and other parts of Australia as already described.

Dr Costin in his discussion on the vegetation of the high moors describes the sequence from dry tussock grassland, savannah woodland, dry sclerophyll, wet sclerophyll, sub-alpine woodland and the herbfields of the highest country. This is paralleled by a rainfall of about twenty inches at the lower levels and one hundred and twenty inches at the high points. The mean annual temperature in the lower grasslands may be 54 deg. F., with Mt Kosciusko at a mean of 36 deg. F.

Only a few interesting plants can be discussed here. There are those of the herbfields, with good soil and more protection, where snow grass and wallaby grass dominate. Snow daisies provide fields of "summer snow" with their white flowers, while gentians and stackhousias add touches of colour. Bogs and fens give swathes of sedges, rushes and tussocks. The Australian edelweiss occurs here and, in the bogs, sphagnum moss. Heathland and feldmark survive, despite the high winds, and have their characteristic plants, with some boronias and mintbushes, as well as the alpine pine, a Podocarpus.

The subalpine woodland has a different look in Tasmania from that on the mainland. In Tasmania, myrtle beeches reach to the treeline, to give a low rainforest, and eucalypts thrive on drier areas. Here also are the various conifers.

On the mainland in Victoria the myrtle beech also occurs in subalpine parts, with higher humidities and more clouds; but it is missing from New South Wales. Snow gums are the best-known feature of the mainland high country. Dr Costin records that the treeline is down to about 5,500 feet on the southern Victorian mountains, to 6,500 feet on Mt Jagungal, and to about 6,000 feet on the Kosciusko plateau.

Alpine woodlands were much more extensive before the coming of the white man and his cattle. Firing the country, with grazing, meant that coppice shoots from the regeneration were cropped. Seedlings were also eaten; and so attempts by the woodland to re-establish were defeated. The process was self-accelerating, since the removal of the woodland gave further exposure to wind and frost.

The attractive open country with its dense grass and herbs retreated downhill.

The term snow gum is used for the fairly widespread white sallee found from northern highlands of New South Wales south into Tasmania; but the true snow gum is a related species found at the highest altitudes, higher than any other tree in Australia. Both species have most attractively patterned bark, and their colouring is enchanced after rain or when given a rub with a handful of snow.

Sphagnum mosses all belong to the same genus, found from the coldest parts of the globe to the tropics. They are highly successful plants, and for that reason the high moors of Australia tend to resemble the tundras of the northern arctic. The vegetative part of the moss can be several inches or up to a yard in length, and absorb tremendous amounts of water. Some species absorb up to twenty times their own weight. The moss is dried and sold for nursery use.

The history of the high country is one of disaster. The Australian Academy of Science prepared a report on the condition of the high mountain catchments. It detailed what had happened through burning, grazing by sheep and cattle, eating out by rabbits and trampling. The dominant grass, a Poa, was not readily eaten by stock, but firing produced more palatable shoots and also opened up the tussocks to penetration by other grasses. However, these were not as good for catchment cover as the Poa.

We have already seen how the woodlands were destroyed. The wet bogs and fens were destroyed by the trampling of cattle, aided in dry years by fire, and many turned into heathlands. About half of these bogs dried out. It is encouraging to know that the overgrazing and firing has now ceased, with the formation of a national park. Some species, thought to have disappeared, have now come back.

Animal life flourishes in these alpine lands. Blood sucking marsh flies are particularly noticeable in high summer. Reports indicate some damage to grassland by casemoth caterpillars, which eat the leaves. The larvae of swift moths feed underground, and between the case moths above, and the swift moths below, grass tussocks may be loosened. If firing and grazing is added the insects may be initially responsible for some erosion. There are a variety of other insects, and in the summer the whole of the high country is invaded by birds. Wedgetails soar in the sky, alert for small mammals, and insect-eating robins and other birds scour the area for food.

Among the outstanding birds are the gang-gang cockatoos and the crimson rosellas. The gang-gangs are grey—the males with vivid red crests. After the first snows these birds can still be seen feeding on the seeds of the snow gums. On the ground crimson rosellas with their scarlet coats stroll along in search of late summer seeding, often in the snow. In the depth of winter the birds move away from the high country into the lower woodlands or even farther afield.

One of the best known of the animals, though rarely seen, is the corroboree frog. Named because of its brilliant black and yellow colouring, it is known to breed in the sphagnum bogs, though possibly this amphibian moves away from the bogs in the winter months, for it has been found under the bark of trees and logs. The eggs are laid in small chambers above the water line of the bogs in the summer, but never near swift-moving streams, which might sweep the tadpoles away.

Common wombats are seen in the alpine woodlands, some wandering across the snow, and where the fall is light breaking through to get the plant food they need. A wombat, deep in its burrow, is unaffected by the chill of winter.

Bibliography

The Australian Environment, fourth edition, edited by G. W. Leeper, C.S.I.R.O., in association with Melbourne University Press.
Atlas of Tasmania, edited by J. L. Davies; Lands and Survey Department, Tasmania.
Flowers and Plants in Victoria, Cochrane, Furher, Rotherham and Willis; A. H. and W. Reed.
Birds of Western Australia, D. L. Serventy and H. M. Whittell; Lamb Publication.
The Last of Lands, edited by L. J. Webb, D. Whitelock, J. Le Gay Brereton; Jacaranda Press.
A Guide to the Native Mammals of Australia, W. D. L. Ride; Oxford.
The Sea-birds of Australia, D. L. and V. N. Serventy, J. Warham; A. H. and A. W. Reed.
Frogs of Western Australia, A. R. Main; W. A. Naturalists' Club.
Waterfowl in Australia, H. J. Frith; Angus and Robertson.
Landforms of Australia, V. N. Serventy; Angus and Robertson.
Dryandra, V. N. Serventy; A. H. and W. Reed.
Wildlife of Australia, V. N. Serventy; Nelson.
Australia's Great Barrier Reef, V. N. Serventy; Georgian House.
State Yearbooks.
Australian Encyclopedia, edited by A. H. Chisholm; Grolier.
Exploring Between Tidemarks, E. Pope and P. McDonald; Australian Museum.
A Guide to Sand Dune Plants, G. G. Smith; W. A. Naturalists' Club.
Wildlife in Australia (magazine); W.L.P.S. of Q.
Australian Natural History (magazine); Australian Museum.

Ecology and change

Ecology is a study of the links between living things and their surroundings. The whole of such interweaving of life in a particular place like a forest or a lake or an estuary is called an ecosystem. If we take our planet earth with its envelopes of water and air, its soil and rocks and all the living things on it, this is called the biosphere.

The term "balance in nature" is an old one and still has its uses so long as we think of it not in a static but in a dynamic way, as a shifting of life round some central point that we have in mind when we say "not so many cicadas this year" or "the fishing is good. Best I've ever known".

Ecology makes such thoughts more exact; but since in any ecosystem there are millions of interactions at all times of the day and night, as well as over the seasons of the year, it is not easy to know exactly what will happen when any particular change made by man takes place. We do know that over long ages of evolution nature has produced a genetic make-up for each creature that allows it a certain amount of adjustment to change in its surroundings.

It must be also realized that individual interactions are parts of long chains of interactions, and a change at one point may cause even more massive changes at some far removed point. We have seen this with DDT when, on its release into the environment often in harmless amounts, it becomes concentrated along food chains to finally prove deadly to an animal species far removed from the original pollution. Such changes are well known; others not so well known. The building of the Aswan Dam to produce power has reduced fish numbers in the Mediterranean, increased the number of water snails that carry disease, and lowered the fertility of the Nile Valley.

Similarly, the building of the St Lawrence Seaway let in the sea lamprey. This devastated the native trout. Smaller fish such as the alewife, with their trout predator removed, increased to huge numbers. So what seemed a fairly harmless change produced disaster for the lakes in commercial and recreational fishing.

In Australia we know how the draining of coastal wetlands for flood mitigation has destroyed the habitat of waterfowl and so reduced their numbers greatly. The building of dams could well reduce the number of barramundi in the north.

The important lesson, however, is not to stop all change but to examine change more carefully in its effect on the whole environment.

Acknowledgements

I am indebted to all those naturalists, amateur and professional, whose research has enabled me to write this book, and particularly to the conservationists who for years, with no payment and no recognition, have fought the conservation battle. Without their continuing work some of the environments I have written about would no longer exist, or would soon be destroyed.

92